A TARGET BOOK

Women with a Cause

Edited, with commentary by Bennett Wayne

GARRARD PUBLISHING COMPANY
CHAMPAIGN, ILLINOIS

Picture credits:

Michael Abramson for Black Star: p. 4
The Bettmann Archive: pp. 17, 70, 74, 98 (both), 103 (all), 117, 131, 139 (bottom left)
The Bostonian Society: p. 54
Brown Brothers: pp. 6, 28, 39, 48, 67, 86, 139 (top left), 147 (both), 158 (top right and bottom)
Culver Pictures: pp. 32, 125, 139 (top right and bottom right), 142, 165
Karsh, Ottawa: p. 134
The Sophia Smith Collection, Smith College: p. 62
Wide World Photos: p. 158 (top left and middle)

Library of Congress Cataloging in Publication Data

Wayne, Bennett.
    Women with a cause.
    (Target series)
    SUMMARY: Biographies of four outstanding women in United States history: Anne Hutchinson, Lucretia Mott, Susan B. Anthony, and Eleanor Roosevelt.
    1. Women—Biography—Juvenile literature. [1. Women—Biography]   I. Wayne, Bennett. II. Title.
HQ1123.W63   920.72 [920]   75-4971
ISBN 0-8116-4914-8

Copyright © 1975 by Garrard Publishing Company
All rights reserved. Manufactured in the U.S.A.

Contents

Women with a Cause.	5
ANNE HUTCHINSON: Defender of Religious Freedom by Doris Faber.	6
LUCRETIA MOTT: Foe of Slavery by Doris Faber.	48
SUSAN B. ANTHONY: Pioneer in Woman's Rights by Helen Stone Peterson.	86
ELEANOR ROOSEVELT: First Lady of the World by Charles P. Graves.	134
Index.	166

Women with a Cause

In the United States in the year 1970, the woman at the left was marching in the cause of equal rights for women. Her sisters of the 1880s had fought for the right to vote; her sisters of the 1920s had won it. Yet, in the second half of the 20th century, women still had not achieved equal rights. Their frustration gave birth to a new women's movement.

This book is about other women of earlier eras whose lives were devoted to bringing about change. The causes they championed were varied, but this they held in common: the conviction that a woman has the right to speak out for those things she believes to be good and true.

Anne Hutchinson insisted on the right to worship as she wished and the right to teach her ideas to others. Lucretia Mott defended the right of slaves to be free and the right of women in the antislavery movement to be heard. Susan B. Anthony devoted her entire life to the struggle for woman's rights. Eleanor Roosevelt first concerned herself with the human rights of Americans. Then she went on to fight for the same rights for all mankind.

Often in fighting for the rights of others these women advanced the cause of equal rights for women too. They were brave, determined, and unusual for their times—a shining example for women today in their battle for an old-new cause.

Anne Hutchinson
Defender of Religious Freedom

by Doris Faber

Copyright © 1970 by Doris Faber as *A Colony Leader: Anne Hutchinson*

1. A Rare Girl

"My brother has hurt his hand," Anne Marbury called out breathlessly. "He fell on a rock, and it cut him to the bone. Quick, hand me a strip of clean linen!"

Will Hutchinson had already stopped his pony cart by the side of the dusty road, for the sight of a young girl running down the steep path from the top of Lookout Hill had surprised him. What could a girl be doing in this lonely spot?

But as soon as he recognized Anne, Will was less surprised. Anne Marbury was always doing or saying something unexpected. She was so very clever with words that although Will was older than Anne, he couldn't help feeling foolish whenever he tried to talk to her.

Part of Will's shyness with Anne came from the fact that his father kept a shop, while her father was a preacher. In England, in 1601, this made a big difference. But for once, Will was glad to be the son of a storekeeper. As soon as she reached the cart, he offered Anne the finest piece of cloth he had.

"That will serve nicely," Anne said. "Now, please, tear it for me. I must hurry to bind Frank's wound."

Poor Will, Anne thought, as she started up the path again, leaving the boy staring silently after her. Why does he never speak? Then she forgot about him in her haste to reach her brother.

But Will was still waiting when she came back down the hill, leading Frank by his unharmed hand. Frank was younger than his sister, and not nearly as tall. Because she was such a sturdy girl, Anne had become used to mothering her small sisters and brothers.

"Oh, I am so glad you waited, Will!" she cried out in some relief. "I fear Frank is feeling weak. It would be kind of you to drive him home in your cart."

"I—I aimed to, Miss," Will managed to say.

When they drew up at the Marbury gate, Anne thanked Will warmly. But she did not linger, because she was too concerned about Frank. Again she forgot Will as she ran to summon her parents.

Fortunately, Frank recovered from his fall with no ill effects, and soon all was as usual for Anne. Every day she helped her mother care for the younger children. She knitted stockings. She studied the Bible with her father.

Anne loved the peaceful little village of Alford, where her family lived. She had been born there, on

July 17, 1591, and she had never known any other home. But as the years passed, she sometimes felt sad.

"What troubles you, daughter?" her father asked her one day when she was fourteen.

Anne spoke up eagerly. "I would be so happy if I could only see some other part of the world," she said.

The Reverend Marbury smiled. "I have news for you," he told her. "We are moving to London!"

2. In London

The bustle of London thrilled Anne.

But she spent very little time out of doors. As the daughter of a respectable family, she could not think of walking the narrow, crowded streets alone. Nobody related to a minister would dream of visiting the playhouse where dramas by one Will Shakespeare were attracting noisy mobs. Still, Anne found excitement enough.

Almost every day friends of her father came to dine at the Marbury table, and their talk fascinated Anne.

Religion was the main point of dispute in London during the early 1600s. People in every walk of life argued about religion, and even fought about religion. With her lively mind, Anne eagerly followed all of the discussion. Should the old, traditional ways of worship be followed? Or were new ways needed?

It was not considered fitting for a girl or woman to take any part in conversation about such serious subjects. But Anne's father never objected if she drew up a stool and sat listening while one minister after another spoke his views.

Then, after the guests departed, the Reverend Marbury would willingly answer his daughter's questions. No other of his ten children was as keen as Anne, he had already decided. So he fell into the habit of speaking frankly to her about his own religious problems.

Anne already knew some of this story, of course. Even as a small child, she had heard about her father's terrible few months in Marshalsea prison.

"Have him to the Marshalsea!" That's what an old bishop had commanded, after hearing young Mr. Marbury criticize some practices of England's church leaders.

In particular, Anne's father had disapproved of letting unworthy men serve as ministers only because they belonged to wealthy families. Yet the Reverend Marbury never went as far as some men in attacking the established ways of conducting church services. Even so, he had been forbidden to preach for several years after his release from jail.

Now he was permitted to preach again, but some

bishops still suspected him. In truth, the Reverend Marbury was growing more and more discontented.

However, before he reached the point of speaking out openly again, he fell sick and died.

Anne was shaken with grief. "What's to become of me now?" she asked herself. If only it were possible for a woman to be a minister! She longed for nothing so much as the chance to take up her father's unfinished task.

But she knew how the very idea of a woman standing up to preach would shock every bishop in the kingdom. So what was she to do?

"You must find a good man and wed him," her mother suggested gently.

With a sad smile, Anne shook her head. "None would have me," she said. "Who would want a wife who longs to be a minister?"

Anne's mother sighed. Truly, the girl was too clever for most men, that was the trouble. So the years passed, and several of Anne's younger brothers and sisters married. All this while, she cheerfully helped her mother at home. And she spent every free moment studying her Bible.

Then, when she was 21, an unexpected visitor called on her. By this time Anne thought of herself as an old maid who would never marry. Indeed it was rare for a woman to find a husband after she had reached such an advanced age.

But Anne didn't look a bit like an old maid when she recognized the man standing at her front door.

"Will Hutchinson!" she cried. "Whatever has brought you to London?" And a warm glow of memories from her country childhood turned her cheeks pink.

Her smiling welcome encouraged Will. He was still too shy to tell her how much he had admired her when she was just a little girl. Nor could he tell her how his heart had leaped when he heard by chance that she was not married. But he could say how glad he was that he had dared to make this trip.

Anne was clearly pleased to see him, and soon her simple pleasure in renewing an old friendship changed into a deeper feeling. She married Will Hutchinson in London on August 9, 1612. Then she moved back to Alford with him.

3. "Thine Eyes Shall See"

A pale little girl was asleep on the grass when Anne Hutchinson came out into her garden one spring morning several years later.

"Wake up, child," she said gently. "Have I not seen you at the farm beyond the old mill? Pray, what is your trouble?"

Still rubbing her eyes, the little girl stood and tried

to curtsy. "It's my ma who needs you, Mistress Hutchinson," she said. "Ma's down with the fever again."

Mrs. Hutchinson nodded. In the time since she'd returned to Alford as Will Hutchinson's wife, she had grown used to being called on like this. All around the countryside, farm wives thought of her when illness struck, because she knew so many healing herbs and also because she had such understanding ways.

Even though she had a new baby of her own every year or two, Anne was always willing to help other families. So she pored over old books till she knew as much about medicines as most doctors did. Because no church would accept a woman minister, she couldn't preach the word of God to heal people's spirits. But at least she could brew potions to heal their bodies.

Still, Mrs. Hutchinson never stopped feeling that religion was the foundation of life. Her faith was so strong that she actually did more than give out herb tea or fever powders. At the farm beyond the old mill, for instance, she saw at once that no medicine could cure the little girl's mother. But Mrs. Hutchinson would not let the poor woman despair.

In addition to doing everything possible to ease her pain, Mrs. Hutchinson also raised her spirits by quietly speaking to her about God's goodness and his love for all those who loved him. Whether she knew it or not, Anne Hutchinson really was preaching the word of God as well as practicing medicine.

But in the quiet of her room, Mrs. Hutchinson's own prayers were more and more troubled. She could never doubt the glory of God, but some of the accepted methods of worshiping him upset her.

A century earlier, in several countries, feelings like those that were distressing Mrs. Hutchinson had brought great changes. Till that time, all of Europe had been united in the Roman Catholic Church. Then some men had protested against the established ways so strongly that large groups of people broke away from the Roman church and formed new churches.

In England, King Henry VIII founded the Church of England at about the same period when other Protestant churches were being founded. However, he acted purely for personal reasons. When he wanted a divorce which the pope in Rome refused to grant him, Henry decided that church affairs in his country must be controlled by its own king.

But should the services in the new church follow the same pattern as in the old days? What sort of robes should clergymen wear? Questions like these had been stirring bitter arguments ever since King Henry's day.

By and large, the other new Protestant churches favored less ceremony than Rome, and they also tried to limit the power of their leaders. In the Church of England, though, many powerful figures fought to hold on to their privileges. Those who disapproved of this, and felt that a more *pure* form of worship was needed, became known as *Puritans*.

After much prayer all alone in her room, Anne Hutchinson became a Puritan.

Taking this step was no light matter. In many parts of England, Puritans were so hated that they had to hold their meetings secretly. Some Puritan families had moved to Holland, but even Holland no longer welcomed them. More and more Puritans were braving the stormy Atlantic to sail all the way to the wilderness of New England.

Mrs. Hutchinson knew what she was risking when she became a Puritan, but she felt that she had to follow her own conscience. Her husband agreed with her, for he still stood in awe of her superior learning. Week after week he drove her to the nearby market town of Boston.

This was a center of Puritanism. Here there were still open meetings led by the Reverend John Cotton, one of the most brilliant speakers in the Puritan cause. Mrs. Hutchinson listened to his sermons, and her spirit rejoiced. At last she had found the teacher she had been seeking!

But hardly had Mrs. Hutchinson found him when he was removed from her sight. He had finally attracted the attention of London bishops who detested Puritanism, and they commanded: "Keep silent!" The Reverend Cotton would not, and he did not want to go to prison. Instead, he boarded a ship bound for a new Boston far across the ocean.

Then Mrs. Hutchinson sat alone in her room again and prayed for guidance. Finally she emerged, holding her Bible in both hands.

It was opened to the chapter containing the words of Isaiah, the prophet. Anne Hutchinson read aloud in her clear and sweet voice:

"Though the Lord give you the bread of adversity, and the water of affliction, yet shall not thy teachers be removed into a corner any more, but *thine eyes shall see thy teachers.*"

Will Hutchinson bowed his head. It would be hard to bid farewell to Alford, to leave his friends and his shop. But he could not stand in his wife's way. If she felt called to follow the Reverend Cotton to distant New England, so be it. He would depart for London at once, to find out when the next ship was sailing!

4. Aboard the *Griffin*

In the summer of 1634, Anne Hutchinson boarded the good ship *Griffin* at a London dock. Her youngest child, Susanna who was barely seven months old, nestled in her arms. Little William was tugging at her skirt as they walked up the gangway.

Then came Will Hutchinson with the older children—Katherine, Mary, Anne, Samuel, Francis, Bridget and Faith. Nineteen-year-old Richard was the last in line.

Edward, who was almost 21, had sailed to America some months earlier with an uncle. They were building a house for the family in the new Boston.

The landing of a shipload of Puritans in the early days of the Massachusetts Bay Colony.

Nobody could tell what dangers might lie ahead. Other women, leaving the world they had always known, looked fearful, but not Anne Hutchinson! The voyage would take only two months, she reminded her family. Then they would be snug and comfortable in their new home.

Yet even a summer crossing of the Atlantic was far from easy, as they all soon discovered. Only a few hours after they set sail, the *Griffin* began bobbing like a cork. The people and the animals aboard became seasick.

For in addition to some two hundred passengers, the ship was also carrying almost as many head of cattle to the New World. There were no separate compartments for this livestock. So everywhere on deck, babies were crying, mothers were feeling seasick, and frightened cows were trying to pull loose the ropes that tied them to the railing.

Even when the ocean turned calmer, and barrels of food could be lifted out of the cargo hold, the cries of the children continued. They could not be satisfied with the dry salted meat that had been taken along for eating on the long voyage. Soon many of the young ones turned weak and feverish; an infant died, and then another.

Only Mrs. Hutchinson seemed able to preserve a hopeful air. "Trust in the goodness of God," she told the mourning mothers. With her firm faith and her friendly ways, Mrs. Hutchinson spread comfort all day long. Her fellow passengers all took heart from her words—except the two ministers aboard.

The Reverend John Lothrop and the Reverend Zachariah Symmes were both strict and severe in their manner. None among the Puritan passengers wore any but the plainest clothes, and yet these two stood out with their black cloaks and their frowning faces. They listened to Mrs. Hutchinson's comforting words, and they shook their heads.

"The woman dares to preach her own ideas!" the Reverend Symmes said to his fellow minister.

"She must be taught a lesson," the Reverend Lothrop answered.

To them, obedience was more important than love. So the next day the Reverend Symmes preached a long sermon warning that anybody who failed to obey the laws of God would be punished severely. He said that no sin, not even a small one, could be forgiven. He also said that the infants who had died aboard the ship were already suffering the terrible torture reserved for all sinners.

Anne Hutchinson listened quietly, but her eyes flashed sparks of fire. As soon as the Reverend Symmes finished, she hurried to his side.

"Mr. Symmes," she said, "why did you frighten those poor women whose babies died? Will you tell me—"

The minister coldly interrupted her. "Mistress Hutchinson," he said, "it is not fitting for you to question me."

Mrs. Hutchinson's face turned pale, but she spoke up once more. "Surely God loves little children," she insisted. "He knows that they cannot understand many things. If a child dies before reaching the age of reason, God would not punish the child."

Mr. Symmes shook his head. "I warn you, Mistress Hutchinson," he said. "The laws of God have been studied by the wisest men, and you must obey them or you will be sorry." Then he left her before she could say another word.

Mrs. Hutchinson stood a moment deep in thought. Was it for this kind of cruel preaching that she had left the safety of Alford? No! But she could not stay angry.

Her dear Mr. Cotton would never preach this way, she told herself, and she turned her mind to the happy day when they would arrive at the new Boston.

Everyone aboard the *Griffin* joined in joyous prayer on the September morning when land was finally sighted. Even the Reverend Symmes and the Reverend Lothrop wore unaccustomed smiles as they gave thanks for their deliverance from the perils of the sea. But after they sailed in closer to the Boston harbor, the happy excitement faded.

Young Richard Hutchinson spoke up for them all. "I don't like the look of this new Boston," he said disgustedly. "It's nothing but a few little huts made of logs!"

For once, his mother could not urge him to look on the bright side. At her own first sight of her new home, even Anne Hutchinson started to weep!

5. New Boston

Mrs. Hutchinson stopped weeping as soon as she spied her oldest son. Edward was standing in the little throng by the waterside waiting to greet the *Griffin*'s passengers. What a grown man he seemed already! And there was Will Hutchinson's brother beside Edward, and other friends from old Boston, including Mr. Cotton.

The sight of her son and her cherished teacher made Mrs. Hutchinson rejoice that she had dared to leave Alford. Of course, she still missed her tidy home there, and her garden with its neat beds of herbs and flowers. But in the next few weeks she quickly grew used to her new surroundings.

As she soon discovered, all around the new Boston was a tangle of salt marsh and woods. Out toward some of the other settlements of the Massachusetts Bay Colony, several families had started farms. These could be seen from the hilltops as tiny islands where man had made a mark in the wilderness. But for all its untamed look, this new land had a grand beauty of its own—and Anne Hutchinson loved it.

Most especially, she loved Boston. Though Edward had built just a log cabin, it did provide ample shelter for the time being. Come spring, Will Hutchinson and his sons would build a stronger house, but there was no cause to worry over that matter. Meanwhile, even the biting east wind and the icy cold of Boston's winter did not distress Mrs. Hutchinson.

Here she felt more fully alive than in old England. But almost all of the other women were frightened by the drastic change in their lives. They had to learn how to cook new foods, such as the Indians' maize, and they had to do without the comforts they had always known. Often, they and their children fell sick.

Then Mrs. Hutchinson was always ready to offer help. After cooking for her own family, she cheerfully boiled another pot of soup for an ailing neighbor. She sat up with feverish mothers and took care of their children.

A young woman named Mary Dyer, who had worked as a hat-maker in London before crossing the ocean, became seriously ill after the birth of her first baby. Mrs. Hutchinson hardly slept till both mother and child were out of danger.

"Do you never tire, Mistress Hutchinson?" Mary Dyer asked her.

Mrs. Hutchinson smiled at the question. "Surely I do, Mary," she answered. "But then the Lord gives me new energy."

Besides doing so much to help other people, Mrs. Hutchinson started a new garden in the spring. Then, after her husband and sons had built a larger house, she was busier than ever. Will Hutchinson had sent to England for supplies, and his wife had one of the biggest houses in the colony.

But busy and content as she was, Mrs. Hutchinson had one worry. Ever since she had been in Boston, she had kept it to herself. She was troubled by the harsh tone of some of the preaching she heard in church. Mr. Cotton still made her heart soar whenever he spoke, but Mr. Cotton shared the pulpit with some other ministers.

In particular, the Reverend John Wilson struck her as a cold and cruel man. He reminded her all too clearly of the Reverend Symmes from the *Griffin*, who was now in charge of a church in an outlying settlement.

When she listened to Mr. Wilson she felt a great urge to stand up and argue with him. Yet she could imagine how her own father would have been shocked by such disrespect. So instead she thought of another plan.

6. Mistress Hutchinson's Meetings

One Monday morning, after an especially gloomy sermon by Mr. Wilson, Mrs. Hutchinson called on Mary Dyer, the young hat-maker. She also visited Jane Hawkins and several other women who had been comforted by her own words of faith.

"Will you come to see me this evening?" Mrs. Hutchinson asked in each house she visited. "I would like to talk about the sermon given yesterday."

Six women came to hear Anne Hutchinson that first Monday evening, and a week later sixty came. Because so many husbands were curious to discover what their wives found of such interest, Mrs. Hutchinson soon began holding a second meeting on Thursday evenings for both men and women. Over a hundred people were present at these gatherings.

What was Mistress Hutchinson up to?

The Reverend Wilson angrily asked the question, and he turned even angrier when he heard the answer.

So this woman had the boldness to criticize his sermons!

No, she was merely *explaining* the sermon preached in church the preceding Sunday, her friends insisted.

"She means no harm," the Reverend Cotton said repeatedly.

"Ah, but she *does* harm," the Reverend Wilson answered.

So Mr. Cotton felt more and more unhappy. Not that he himself was completely in sympathy with Mr. Wilson's stern views, but he preferred smoothing over differences rather than making an issue about them. And he advised Mrs. Hutchinson to do the same.

Now it was her turn to feel unhappy. Would Mr. Cotton truly wish her to go against her own conscience?

No, certainly not, he said warmly.

Then if her conscience told her that she must keep on with her meetings, how could she stop them?

Mr. Cotton sighed. "I fear trouble ahead," he said. And he was right. Within just a few months, the biggest storm in the history of Massachusetts Bay Colony burst over Anne Hutchinson's head.

7. Sound and Fury

"This woman threatens our church!"

"She threatens our state!"

"She threatens both our church and our state!"

In Boston's shops and at its dinner tables, and in every village in the Massachusetts Bay Colony, angry ministers argued this way against allowing Anne Hutchinson to continue her meetings.

Those who said that she was really a double threat —to the established church and to the legal government of the colony—had good reason for their concern. For Massachusetts Bay was not a democracy during its early days. It was a theocracy.

This meant that the church and the state were so closely bound together that, in effect, they made one single governing body. Only Puritans could vote or hold office, and no other religious group was allowed within the colony's borders. On every sort of matter, the will of the church was enforced by law.

For instance, when it turned out that some of the Puritan women liked to dress up a bit on special occasions, the strict ministers were disturbed. So they asked the colony's ruling council to consider this question, and a new law was passed forbidding any use of lace to trim a gown.

To the Reverend Wilson and all those who thought along the same lines, Anne Hutchinson's offense was much worse than merely wearing lace.

They sincerely believed that life was a terrible contest between the forces of good and evil, and that most people were too weak to escape being tempted by the devil. So the sternest rules were needed to thwart Satan—rules that everybody had to obey. The Reverend Wilson was afraid of allowing any individual freedom.

Although Mrs. Hutchinson's meetings gave hope

and comfort to so many people, even some of her friends could see the danger of permitting them to continue. "If Mistress Hutchinson can say what she wishes, then why can't every Tom, Dick, and Harry hold meetings too?" they asked. No, that would surely cause problems, many people agreed.

The young governor of the colony, Henry Vane, and a few other forward-thinking people were much less fearful. They tried to convince their fellow citizens that no real harm would come of allowing free discussion. "Let everybody speak," they said. "A peaceful discussion will help to clear up many issues and make us stronger in the long run."

"Ah, but how can we keep the peace if the ignorant are free to debate with the wisest men?" the Reverend Wilson demanded. "I promise you armed uprisings unless this woman is silenced."

Armed uprisings! The mere words struck terror in many hearts. All through history there were frightening instances of religious warfare. Could this happen in Massachusetts?

Shivering at the very thought, many good people turned their backs on Anne Hutchinson. They voted against delegates to the lawmaking assembly who supported her right to speak, and they even threw Governor Vane out of office. They restored their old governor, John Winthrop, to power—and that was a bad omen for Mrs. Hutchinson.

John Winthrop (left) and Mr. Wilson were determined to silence Mrs. Hutchinson and her followers.

Governor Winthrop hated Vane, and he disliked anybody who was as friendly with Vane as Mrs. Hutchinson had been. So Governor Winthrop lost no time in discussing Mrs. Hutchinson's case with the Reverend Wilson. They decided that the best way to proceed would be to turn the woman's remaining supporters against her. Within the next few weeks, many of them were arrested.

They were charged with being guilty of all sorts of "errors" in their own religious views. But the words used to explain their crimes were so confusing that none of the accused could defend themselves.

Even so, they were punished severely. One minister who had spoken up in favor of Mrs. Hutchinson was banished. Some of her neighbors who had signed a petition supporting her had their property taken away or lost the right to vote. Then many of Mrs. Hutchinson's former friends changed their minds, and others who still felt that she was right became afraid to say this openly.

Meanwhile, long sermons about religious "errors" were delivered from almost every pulpit in Massachusetts. The name of the offending woman was on every tongue. But in all the sound and fury over Anne Hutchinson's meetings, one fact was forgotten.

It was the fact that the Puritans of Massachusetts had left England and settled in this new land because they craved religious freedom for themselves. They well knew how it felt to be prevented from worshiping God in their own way. Still they were not yet ready to do unto others as they wished others to do unto them. And so, on November 7, 1637, they summoned Anne Hutchinson into court.

8. The Trial

It was a cold day when Mistress Anne Hutchinson stood up to defend herself before the highest officials of the Massachusetts Bay Colony.

There was no heat in the bare and unlit courtroom. Mrs. Hutchinson had reached the age of 46 and her health was no longer what it had been. In a few months, she would give birth to her fourteenth child. Yet she stood straight and tall, still giving the appearance of being a strong woman.

Governor Winthrop himself opened the case against her.

"Mistress Hutchinson," he said, "you are called here as one of those that have troubled the peace of the commonwealth and the churches."

Every bench was filled with solemn-faced men. Many of them nodded approvingly as Governor Winthrop went on:

"You have spoken many things, as we have been informed, very damaging to the honor of the churches and the ministers thereof."

No sound broke the silence, but the governor's sharp voice grew louder.

"You have maintained a meeting in your house," he said, "and this has been condemned by the general assembly as a thing not permitted, but still you have continued the same."

Governor Winthrop paused, then said slowly: "Therefore, we have summoned you so that we may either rescue you and make you a profitable member among us or, if you be stubborn, take such action that you may trouble us no longer."

Anne Hutchinson did not turn pale. She knew that she faced being sent away from Massachusetts Bay. That was the punishment for all those who would not be led by the opinions of the leading clergymen. Two years earlier, Roger Williams of Salem had been exiled. Others had suffered the same fate. If it was God's will that she be ordered to leave Boston, then perhaps she and her family might journey southward, to join Williams in Rhode Island.

But Mrs. Hutchinson was not ready to give up her cause without fighting for it. She had neither friend nor lawyer to speak up for her in this court. Governor Winthrop and the Reverend Wilson had seen to it that none of her supporters were admitted. Not even her husband or her sons had been given permission to be present. Still Mrs. Hutchinson felt fully capable of speaking for herself.

During a whole long day, and then another, she did just that. No matter how Governor Winthrop battered at her, she would not admit that she had erred.

"I am called here to answer before you," she told him repeatedly, "but what is the charge against me?"

"I have told you already," Governor Winthrop said impatiently. "What more can I do?"

"Name one charge, I pray you."

Then the governor would confer with the Reverend Wilson and after a moment inform her that she had sinned by slandering clergymen. Did she not hold the ministers of the colony in error on this fine point, or that fine point, in one sermon or another?

But instead of falling into the trap of disputing with the ministers who testified against her, Mrs. Hutchinson kept insisting on her own right to express her faith in God's goodness.

"What gives you that right?" Governor Winthrop finally demanded.

"That's a matter of conscience, sir."

Then Governor Winthrop lost his temper.

"You must control your conscience," he snapped at her, "or it will have to be controlled for you."

Anne Hutchinson demands to be told the charges of the court.

Still the hearing droned on with one black-cloaked minister after another testifying how seriously Mistress Hutchinson had erred. Even her dear teacher Mr. Cotton could not help her, although he tried. Though she meant well, he finally said sadly, it was nevertheless clear that she was misguided.

For two whole days, the proceedings continued, but in this strange sort of court Governor Winthrop was both the chief accuser and the chief judge. His decision could be in no doubt.

Knowing this all along, Anne Hutchinson had still hoped that she might win her case by the simple truth of her defense. She was upholding the principle of freedom of conscience, and sooner or later it must triumph. But its time had not yet come in 1637.

So after two long, cold days in court, Mrs. Hutchinson was sentenced to be sent away from the Massachusetts Bay Colony.

In an odd show of mercy, Governor Winthrop added one further condition. Because the winter snows would make travel through the wilderness so difficult, there would be a delay of four months in imposing the court's verdict. But during these months the accused was to be imprisoned in the home of some high-minded minister, who would do everything possible to bring her to see the error of her ways. Anne Hutchinson heard the verdict without flinching.

9. A Bitter Winter

Many times during that winter, Mrs. Hutchinson wished that she had been sent out into the wilderness right after her trial. Surely the worst snowstorm, or even the most violent Indian attack, could not have added to her suffering. The cruelty she endured in her imprisonment was harder to bear, she thought.

For she was kept during these months in the home of a stern friend of the Reverend Wilson. Neither her husband nor her children could visit her. But a whole host of black-coated enemies tormented her every day.

"Mistress Hutchinson, admit your errors," the Reverend Symmes insisted, shaking his bony finger as if to cast some spell upon her.

"Cease your evil ways, before it is too late," another angry minister warned her.

Though it was clear that her health was failing, they all kept hounding her unmercifully. And yet, by their own lights, they were being kind to her. They truly believed they were offering her one last opportunity to escape the devil.

According to their way of thinking, any person who dared to defy them deserved worse punishment than merely being sent away. Even in the wilderness, this sinner would still be a member of the Boston church, and would thereby be protected at least in some measure from Satan, they reasoned. So, unless she could be led to see how wrong her ideas were, a further step would be necessary. They would have to go through the fearful ceremony of casting her out of the church.

To avoid this terrible step, these ministers kept tirelessly buzzing around Mrs. Hutchinson, and accusing her, and attacking her. Under the continuous pounding, she grew weaker every day. At last, almost fainting with weariness, she finally did admit that she had erred in one respect.

"Doubtless I have taken too much upon myself," she said in a low voice.

"Ah!" the Reverend Symmes exclaimed. "You have indeed been puffed up with a sense of your own importance. You are guilty of the sin of pride. Now you must beg forgiveness, and be proud no more, woman."

Anne Hutchinson bowed her head silently.

She could go no further. She could not promise the Reverend Symmes to give up listening to her own conscience. No, she must be free to worship as she chose.

The Reverend Wilson was not satisfied. So on March 15 he summoned the members of the Boston church to attend the most solemn gathering ever held in the Massachusetts Bay Colony. Every bench was filled, and among those present this time were some members of Mrs. Hutchinson's family as well as many of the people who had attended her meetings.

But the loyal Will Hutchinson was nowhere to be seen. He had been sure that his wife would be forced to leave the colony. So, with a party of nineteen trusted men, including his own grown sons, he had gone into the wilderness some weeks earlier to search for a place where they could build a new settlement. They hoped to find some suitable land near Roger Williams in Rhode Island.

Among those who did come to the meeting, some had already suffered for supporting Mrs. Hutchinson. But one man was still brave enough to rise in an attempt to defend her. Before he could speak a word, the Reverend Wilson declared him out of order.

Then the minister coldly called for Mistress Hutchinson to be led in to hear the awful penalty she had brought upon herself.

There were gasps of surprise and pity as Anne Hutchinson walked into the crowded church. Many eyes filled with tears. For the tall and strong woman they remembered had changed sadly during her imprisonment. That she would very soon give birth to a baby was obvious from her slow and heavy step, but her pale face had changed even more than her figure. Lines of pain and sorrow showed how she had been suffering. She looked very ill.

But she stood in patient silence when the Reverend Wilson stepped forward again. Then he spoke.

"Mistress Anne Hutchinson," he said, "in the name of the Lord Jesus Christ, I do not only pronounce you worthy to be cast out, but I do cast you out. . . . And in the name of Christ I do deliver you up to Satan. . . . Therefore I command you . . . to withdraw yourself out of this congregation."

10. Aquidneck

By now Will Hutchinson had found a likely piece of land in Rhode Island and he was building a log cabin there. And his oldest son, Edward, was hurrying back through the wilderness all alone.

Fortunately, Edward arrived in Boston just in time to be with his mother when the Reverend Wilson spoke his dreadful sentence. Anne Hutchinson leaned on her son's arm as she walked slowly out of the church. All who were present bowed their heads in silence while these two departed.

Not even stopping to rest, Edward then went to gather up his younger brothers and sisters, who had been staying with trusted friends. A dozen of these good friends who could not be frightened out of their love for Mrs. Hutchinson had already decided to join the family in its exile.

"Make haste!" Edward kept urging. He had

promised his father to do his best to prevent further trouble from Governor Winthrop.

So they quickly packed only the most necessary food and clothing, no more than they could carry themselves. And they set forth the day after the Reverend Wilson pronounced his sentence.

Mrs. Hutchinson was glad to leave Boston. Though she had spent a few happy years there, she thought that its air was no longer fit for breathing. Until its leaders learned to allow more freedom, she had no wish to see the town again.

As for her being forbidden church membership, she felt relieved now that her own conscience really was her only guide. Let the Reverend Wilson do his worst, she need not worry. Now she could worship God in her own way, and she was sure he would not cast out any who loved him.

Thus, her spirit knew more peace than it had in many months. But Mrs. Hutchinson's hardships were far from ended. Winter lingered late that year and the travelers stopped to wait for better weather at a farm kept by relatives outside of Boston. But the air was still frosty when they had to resume their journey.

Because there were no roads through the deep woods they had to cross, they traveled by foot. Weak as she was, for six days Mrs. Hutchinson walked through trackless forest. She slept six nights on the

Anne finds a haven in Rhode Island.

frozen ground. Then when she was close to collapse, they arrived at the Providence settlement started by Roger Williams.

Fortunately, she did not have much farther to go. The place Will Hutchinson had selected as their new home was on a green island the Indians called Aquidneck, not more than a good day's journey from Providence. But when Mrs. Hutchinson arrived at Aquidneck, she hardly had the breath left to greet her husband.

"I fear she will not live much longer," Edward sadly told his father.

Within just a few weeks, Mrs. Hutchinson gave birth to the baby she was expecting. The infant was born dead, and it seemed that the mother would also die. For several months, she was too ill to rise from the rude bed Will Hutchinson had built for her.

During this time the news of her baby's death and her own illness was brought back to Boston. Governor Winthrop shook his head knowingly. "The woman is being punished by God for sinning," he said. Even some of her old friends believed him and shivered.

But as the months passed, Mrs. Hutchinson slowly regained at least some of her old strength. She could begin taking an interest in this new place the Lord had spared her to see. Aquidneck was blessed by nature with a mild climate and grand rocky cliffs overlooking the blue water. The handful of families who had come there in freedom did not envy any other people anywhere in the world.

Anne Hutchinson no longer felt strong enough to preach to her friends and neighbors, but she took comfort in small meetings at which all present prayed silently, or else spoke in turn if they were moved to do so. By choice, the people of Aquidneck built no church, preferring to hold their prayer meetings in each other's houses.

After several years, life in this untroubled wilderness healed Mrs. Hutchinson's spirit, and she looked forward to growing old peacefully there. Then suddenly her calm was shattered. In the spring of 1642 her dear husband, who was 56 years old, became ill. Within a few days, he was dead.

11. A New Start

After her husband died, Mrs. Hutchinson would have liked to have remained the rest of her life in the farmhouse he had built. Her older children were already married, and several had settled near her or in Providence. So she had willing hands to help her run the farm and care for the younger children still at home.

She had also found a new interest since regaining her health. A tribe of friendly Indians was taking up much of her attention. These Indians were already living on Aquidneck when the settlers from Boston arrived.

"You must remember that they can be dangerous," Mrs. Hutchinson's sons warned her.

She shook her head gently. "They are God's creatures as we are," she answered.

She believed she could help these fellow men by teaching them something about her medicines made of common herbs and about her own religious faith. She spent many happy hours visiting with the Indians.

But during the months following her husband's death, there were more and more signs that she might not be allowed to remain undisturbed in her wilderness retreat. Since the founding of Providence and other settlements that would soon be combined to make up the colony of Rhode Island, the leaders of the Massachusetts Bay Colony had been claiming that all this land really belonged to Massachusetts.

Because travel was so difficult, not much had been done to back up this claim. However, the existence of a few settlements which refused to recognize the authority of ministers like the Reverend Wilson increasingly struck strict Puritans as a threat. They began sending messengers southward, ordering the rebellious settlers to mend their ways.

When all of these messages were disregarded, Massachusetts became even more concerned. It seemed possible that armed soldiers might be sent out any day, to take over the wilderness area by force.

Fearing not so much for her own safety as for that of her children, Mrs. Hutchinson decided to move still farther to the south.

Below New England, in the Dutch colony of New Netherland, she would be able to worship as she pleased without any interference from Massachusetts. That's where she would go!

Late in the summer of 1642, Mrs. Hutchinson left

Aquidneck with most of her family. Thirty-five other Rhode Island families joined her on her new pilgrimage to escape religious persecution.

This journey was longer than her flight from Boston, but less difficult. In fine weather, and with sandy meadow instead of deep forest along most of their route, they were able to drive their cattle easily, and even bring wagons carrying household goods. Much of the time they stayed right in sight of the blue waters of Long Island Sound, which greatly pleased Mrs. Hutchinson, for she loved to look out over the water.

So she was more than happy when the men of the party picked out a tract of land for their new homes bordering on this same calm body of water. Her own farm extended inland to a small stream. None of this area had yet been settled by the Dutch, though it lay safely within their territory. In years to come, it would be called Westchester County, and the small stream would be known as the Hutchinson River.

Dutch officials farther south in New Amsterdam willingly gave permission for the new settlement when several of the men from Aquidneck called upon them. But a serious problem soon arose. On the morning the men returned from New Amsterdam and began chopping down trees to use for building log cabins, Indians with fierce streaks of red painted on their faces gathered on the beach.

These were members of a tribe which had already learned to distrust white men. Other land of theirs had been taken from them without fair payment, and they had been promised that they would not be disturbed in this area. Now it seemed to them that another promise was about to be broken.

So the Indians advanced and stood in a circle around the white men who were cutting a tree trunk into logs.

All of the Aquidneck women and children were camped nearby. They saw the Indians advance, and they saw that their own men kept right on cutting down trees.

"These Indians mean no harm," Mrs. Hutchinson said in her clear voice. Remembering how she had made friends with the Aquidneck Indians, she thought she would do the same in this new place. But these Indians seemed far less willing to accept her friendship.

As she stepped forward, their leader also took a step, and he made signs with his hands that had an unmistakable meaning. Go away, he gestured. Go away!

Then he turned and led his followers back toward the beach. Fearful murmurs arose among the Aquidneck women and children.

"All will be well!" Mrs. Hutchinson said calmly. If only she were right!

12. Unheeded Warning

After that first frightening moment, the new community had no real trouble from the Indians for a full year. It seemed that Mrs. Hutchinson was, after all, succeeding in making friends with them.

"They are all God's creatures," she would remind her fellow settlers. "Treat them fairly, and there is no reason to fear them."

Mrs. Hutchinson's youngest child, her daughter Susanna, took her mother's assurances as the simple truth. Even when an Indian brave turned up at their door one day with red paint striping his cheeks—a sight the settlers hadn't seen since their arrival—Susanna teased him into running a race with her down to the beach.

Susanna, who was eight years old, had never learned to be afraid of any Indian.

But many of the older settlers could hardly hide their alarm at the sight of the war paint. From passing travelers, they had heard how some of the Indians in other parts of the Dutch territory had already gone on the warpath because still more of their land had been taken from them. Whole families of settlers had been killed.

Surely this one painted Indian had come intending to give Mrs. Hutchinson some sort of warning that the Aquidneck party faced the same fate. But Mrs.

Hutchinson herself refused to believe trouble was coming.

Most of her neighbors could not share her calm faith. They gathered up their families and hurried down to New Amsterdam to seek refuge in the Dutch fort there. So they escaped the terrible wrath of the Indians.

On a cloudless day in September of 1643, a band of Indians swept up from the beach with their faces painted fiery red. In their hands were tomahawks. They went first to the house of an Aquidneck family named Throgmorton, who had chosen not to flee southward. The Indians killed every member of that family, butchered its cattle, and set its house ablaze.

On that same September afternoon, they killed Mrs. Hutchinson and her whole family.

Only little Susanna escaped. The Indian brave she had played with took pity on her and adopted her as his own daughter. Otherwise, burned ashes were all that remained of the whole Aquidneck settlement, and these were soon scattered by the wind. Nobody has ever discovered exactly where Anne Hutchinson met her fearful death.

But she has not been forgotten. Because she made such a brave stand in defense of religious freedom, Anne Hutchinson has come to be regarded as one of the outstanding figures in American history.

The Massachusetts Puritans who cast her out did

not see the error of their own ways so quickly. Some, like the Reverend Wilson, even said that Mrs. Hutchinson's cruel death was proof that she had offended God. They kept on doing all they could to keep other people from following their own consciences.

It took many years before religious persecution ended in New England. During those years, others besides Anne Hutchinson suffered for daring to worship God in their own way. Mrs. Hutchinson's young friend Mary Dyer was one of these. For preaching the new Quaker doctrine, which was very much like the religious ideas Mrs. Hutchinson had been working out all by herself, Mary Dyer was hanged in Boston by the Puritans.

Then, as the years passed, Boston learned to value freedom of religion as highly as political freedom. Although Massachusetts had banished Anne Hutchinson from its borders, it came to be very proud of her. Now a statue of her, holding her Bible in one hand and leading a little child with the other, watches over the front entrance to the Massachusetts State House.

Lucretia Mott
Foe of Slavery

by Doris Faber

Copyright © 1971 by Doris Faber

1. "A Ship! A Ship!"

Lucretia Coffin looked fondly at her two sisters. Sarah was two years older; Eliza was almost two years younger. But they both thought she, Lucretia, should give their father the farewell present they had all made for him.

So Lucretia stepped forward on the dock where last-minute preparations were being hurried. As soon as the tide changed, Captain Thomas Coffin's ship was going to sail. It was the spring of 1800. He was one of the brave New Englanders who had begun trading with far-off China.

"Can you stop a minute?" Lucretia asked, gently pulling at her father's arm. "We have something for you. It's to remind you we'll be counting the days till you return."

Captain Coffin was a tall, strong man whose face was tanned by the sun and wind. Now suddenly he seemed about to weep as he bent down and hugged his middle daughter.

Lucretia felt tears filling her own eyes. Still, she tried to smile. She handed him the bit of sewing the girls had worked on together. With neat stitches they had made a simple sort of calendar for two years. It would probably be that long before they saw him again.

"Thank you, my dear," Captain Coffin said warmly. "Thank you, Sarah and Eliza. Now here's your mother with your brother. Let me kiss each of you. Then I must go aboard."

Before long the ship had sailed, and the excitement of waving good-bye was over. Lucretia tried hard to hide her sadness. With her mother and sisters and little Tom, who was just three years old, she walked up the cobbled streets of Nantucket. Soon they reached their home. It was a white-frame cottage with a neat garden around it.

Nantucket is a small island about 30 miles off the mainland of Massachusetts. Lucretia had been born there on January 3, 1793. Her whole family, back to her great-grandfather, had lived on Nantucket. Many of the island's men were sailors on whaling ships or trading ships.

So the women and children of Nantucket learned to take care of themselves. After Captain Coffin left for China, Lucretia's mother started a small shop in their front parlor. Now she could earn some money while her husband was gone.

One summer morning Mrs. Coffin was busy in her shop. Sarah and Eliza were cleaning the house.

Lucretia took Tom to gather beach plums. On their return, she began cooking a pot of jam.

"Lu, sing me a song," Tom begged.

Lucretia put down her spoon and drew in a deep breath. She sang: "Sing, sing, what shall I sing? The cat's run away with the pudding-bag string!"

Their mother opened the door from her shop. "Oh, Lucretia!" she said. "If you were as far out of town as you are out of tune, you wouldn't get home tonight."

Lucretia laughed, then her sweet face became thoughtful. "Mama, would you rather I stopped trying to sing?" she asked. There was a good reason for the question.

The Coffins and their neighbors were all members of the same religious group. They were Quakers. Their praying was direct and simple, and they tried to live as simply as possible. They wore plain gray or brown clothing every day. Some Quakers did not even approve of music.

Still, Lucretia saw no harm in singing. She thought that she should be able to decide about a matter like this.

Mrs. Coffin seemed to sense this. "Child," she said, "sing if you wish."

Lucretia broke into a smile again. From then on, she hummed softly as she sat knitting socks for Tom. She sang while she walked to school with Sarah and

Eliza. When spring came again, she made her sisters laugh by imitating the songs of the birds sitting on the chimney.

Lucretia did not know that some people thought Quakers never enjoyed themselves. She had a cheerful nature, and she was part of a happy family. She loved Nantucket—its cobbled streets, its busy waterfront, and its windswept beaches. However, she did have a secret worry.

Suppose her father's ship met trouble? Suppose it were lost at sea?

Month after month passed, and she prayed for him nightly. When two years had gone by without any word, Lucretia still did not speak of her fears. Instead, she did all she could to cheer her mother and her sisters.

"Would you like me to recite the entire multiplication table *backwards*?" she would ask if someone looked sad.

Even Lucretia lost heart, though, when three whole years had passed and her father had not returned.

Then on a beautiful spring morning, the cry arose: "A ship! A ship!"

This time Lucretia was not disappointed. Only a few hours later Captain Coffin walked down the gangplank and rushed to throw his arms around his waiting family.

2. Boston

"I have news for you," Captain Coffin said at the dinner table a few weeks later.

Lucretia put down her spoon. What was her father planning? He had just come back from a short trip to Boston. Would he be sailing soon on a ship from that city?

"No, I will not leave you again," Captain Coffin told his family with a smile. "I have had enough of the sea. Now I hope to be a merchant. As soon as I can make the necessary arrangements, we are moving to Boston."

Lucretia clapped a hand to her mouth. Visiting Boston was the most wonderful thing she could think of. However, living there meant no more happy days on Nantucket. How could she give up the only home she had ever known?

These thoughts kept returning to Lucretia during the next few months. While her father looked after business matters, she and her sisters helped their mother pack. Then as moving day drew closer, the girls could not hold back their tears.

Still, Lucretia's first sight of Boston almost made up for all the sadness. As she stepped off the bobbing little ship, she stared in amazement at streets filled with carts and wagons. More people than she had ever imagined crowded the sidewalks.

Dock Square in Boston. Lucretia was eleven when her family moved to the bustling seaport city.

Many things in Boston surprised Lucretia. The greatest surprise was a red-brick schoolhouse around the corner from the Coffins' new home. Both boys and girls were taught there. There had been no school on Nantucket—only a lady who gave lessons to a few pupils in her front parlor.

For more than a year, Lucretia went to this new school with her sisters. Then she began to feel restless. She did not like to trouble her parents, but she thought she had learned all she could there. Happily, her father felt the same way.

"Lucretia," he said one evening after he had listened to her recite a long poem by heart, "I believe you have a keen mind. I think you should be given the chance for more education."

"I would like that," she said quickly.

"Unfortunately, only a few schools offer advanced work to girls," he went on. "None of these is in Boston. However, I have written to find out about a school some Quakers have started in New York State. Would you be willing to leave your family to go there?"

Lucretia gasped. She was not sure. However, she was nearly thirteen. The idea of stepping out into the world pleased her.

"I—I would like to go there," she said.

3. Nine Partners

"Step carefully," Captain Coffin warned.

Lucretia held her long gray skirt a little above her ankles and climbed into the coach. She and her father were starting on the long ride to New York State. The trip would take at least 30 hours, without counting stops where the horses would be changed.

How that coach bounced! Lucretia slept part of the time, but she was very tired when they finally arrived at the school. It was a large, square building set in a park.

"I—I am sure I'm going to like it here," Lucretia said bravely. Yet she already felt lonesome.

Her first weeks at boarding school were the worst she had ever known. After her father left, she missed her family every minute of the day. Often at night her pillow was wet with tears.

Yet, sitting in her classes, she looked calm. No one could have guessed how homesick she was. Although slim and not very tall, she looked older than she really was.

Gradually Lucretia started to feel at home at the Nine Partners School. Its odd name came from the fact that nine men had once owned this land in the Hudson River's green valley. Lucretia liked the school much more after she had made friends with the golden-haired girl who sat next to her in English class.

"You don't seem lonely," the girl said. "Yet I think you must be. All new girls are. Won't you be friends with me? My name is Sarah Mott."

Lucretia smiled. "I have a sister named Sarah at home," she said. The thought of home almost made her burst into tears.

"Let me be your sister while you're here," Sarah Mott whispered as the teacher entered the room.

Before long Lucretia and Sarah did become almost as close as sisters. Because travel to Boston was so difficult, Lucretia spent school vacations visiting Sarah's family in New York State. When she was thirteen, she met Sarah's brother James, who was eighteen. A year later James became a teacher in the boys' school.

Boys were taught in one part of the Nine Partners School, and girls in another. They were not supposed to play with one another. However, Lucretia once crossed over to the boys' side to help a boy who was being punished by being kept in his room without food. She smuggled bread and milk to him.

Sometimes Lucretia managed to talk to Sarah's brother James over the fence which separated the boys' and girls' playgrounds. Although James seemed rather shy, Lucretia enjoyed asking him questions. Soon he felt at ease with her.

"Is it fair that school fees are the same for boys and girls, although boys are taught more subjects? Why can't girls study the same things as boys?" Lucretia asked James these questions, and he thought about them.

"Yes," he decided, "girls should be allowed to study the same subjects."

"Is it not possible for a girl to become a good teacher?" she asked.

James thought about this too. Then he said that a girl might surely turn into a fine teacher.

At sixteen, Lucretia herself was offered the job of assistant teacher in the girls' school. Her first thought, even before writing home to her parents, was to ask James what he thought about the offer.

"I would be pleased if you became a teacher here," he said in his most serious tone. There was a smile about his eyes, though, that Lucretia could not understand.

A few months later, when the term was almost ended, Lucretia asked him another question.

"Do you think it is right," she said, "that I am not being paid for my work? Even the head of the girls' school earns only $20 a term. Yet you and the other men teachers are paid much more."

They were walking in the garden, and nobody else was in sight. James suddenly reached down and took Lucretia's hand.

"No, I think that is wrong," he said. "But I beg you not to worry about it now. You ought not to plan to be a teacher much longer. I would like you to become my wife."

Lucretia was so surprised that, for once, she could not say a word. Still, she nodded her head in happy agreement with this wonderful idea.

4. A New Name

"I, Lucretia, take thee, James Mott, to be my husband," the eighteen-year-old bride said happily. It was April 10, 1811, Lucretia and James's wedding day, in the Pine Street Meeting House in Philadelphia.

Captain Coffin had moved his family to this city

to make a fresh start in business. When the captain's new nail factory and store in Philadelphia began to do well, he sent for James Mott to help him. Soon after, Lucretia and James were married.

The former sea captain was happy to have James Mott for a son-in-law. He also thought James had a good head for business, so he asked him to be his partner. The new sign hanging over his warehouse near Philadelphia's waterfront read "Coffin and Mott —Merchants."

While James and her father worked together, the new Mrs. Mott happily began housekeeping. She and James lived in a few small rooms in a narrow old brick building. It was around the corner from the larger house where the rest of Lucretia's family lived.

"I cannot tell you how pleased I am to be close to you again," she kept telling her mother and sisters.

The year after her marriage, young Mrs. Mott gave birth to a daughter. The baby was named Anna after Mrs. Coffin. Two years later Lucretia had a son, Thomas, named for his grandfather.

Mrs. Mott loved playing games with her children. She taught them to read as soon as they were old enough. She also taught other children in a school for girls which she and a cousin ran for a time.

When her sisters married she helped them get settled in their new homes. These were happy years for her. Then suddenly her father became ill with typhus fever and died. Lucretia did all she could to comfort her mother.

A few years later another fever struck Mrs. Mott's own household. Her three-year-old son became ill, and no medicine seemed to help him. Within a week he died.

Mrs. Mott felt so sad about his death that she herself became ill. When she finally did get well again, she was a more serious person. She turned to religion and spent long hours alone reading her Bible. Then she came to a surprising decision.

"Lucretia has taken up the preaching line," her mother wrote to relatives.

Although there were no women ministers in other religious groups, the Quakers did have some. Any member who felt the call could become a minister, if a committee of elders approved. When Lucretia Mott was 28, she became a minister and spoke at several of the Quaker meeting houses in and around Philadelphia.

Mrs. Mott also kept a lively interest in the world around her. When a man named Benjamin Lundy called a meeting to talk about slavery, she went to hear him speak. This was a great turning point in her life.

Lundy had just come back from a visit to Virginia. There he had been shocked by the sight of a slave market. He had heard the terrible cries of black children who were being taken from their parents. He decided to spend the rest of his life doing all he could to end slavery.

Lucretia Mott was deeply moved by Lundy's words. Like many other Quakers, she had already come to feel that slavery was wrong. Now she spoke to her husband, who had become a cotton merchant.

"James," she said, "I do not think you should continue to sell cotton goods. They have been made with the labor of slaves. I would rather go hungry than earn money from the suffering of others."

James Mott listened to her thoughtfully. He agreed with Lucretia, but he worried about earning enough money to support his family. Finally he decided to do as Lucretia suggested.

As a result, Mr. Mott soon left the cotton trade. He began to sell only woolen goods in his new store on Front Street. Still Mrs. Mott did not think she had done enough. She got a group of wives together. "We must promise each other to stop buying things made by the labor of slaves," she said.

5. Speaking Up

As time went by, Mrs. Mott had four more babies. Three of them were girls named Maria, Elizabeth, and Martha. She also had a son named Thomas, in memory of the boy who had died.

Some of the members of the Pennsylvania Anti-Slavery Society. Lucretia and James Mott are seated in the front row, far right.

"I'm busy as a beaver," she wrote to one of her married sisters. Mrs. Mott kept her house tidy and took care of her children.

She also spoke every week at Quaker meetings. When her children grew older and needed her less, she spent more of her time fighting slavery.

The Motts now had a large house with a comfortable parlor. Here Mrs. Mott welcomed company almost every evening.

"The millions of slaves in our land are the most badly treated group in this country," she would say in her clear, sweet voice. "I feel bound to do all in my power to win freedom for them."

Then she would tell her visitors about the new antislavery society she was helping to plan. Its members were going to hold public meetings against slavery. They would also publish books and newspapers. Their aim would be to convince as many people as possible that slavery ought to be outlawed.

"Similar groups are being formed in other cities in the North," Mrs. Mott would add. "Indeed, a man from Boston hopes to unite them into one group."

His name was William Lloyd Garrison. Unlike Mrs. Mott, and her husband who was quietly encouraging her, Garrison liked to upset people.

"I will be heard!" he shouted. He forced people to pay attention to a problem they had been trying to ignore. Most Northerners still thought that Southern people should decide for themselves whether or not there would be slaves. Garrison did not agree with this. Instead, he said that Northerners had to make Southerners understand that slavery was wrong.

Mrs. Mott felt just the way he did. However, she never shouted at people who did not agree with her. Instead she tried to reason with them. She even read them a simple little verse:

> *If slavery comes by color,*
>   *which God gave,*
> *Fashion may change,*
>   *and you become the slave.*

Still, she helped Mr. Garrison in many ways. In 1833 he decided to call a national meeting of anti-slavery societies. It was to be held in Philadelphia. She told him to use her house as his home away from home. She also did something that was far more daring.

Mrs. Mott took a seat at the back of the hall on the day the meeting started. With her were a few dozen other women, most of them Quakers. Like her, they had been working to make this gathering a success. However, it was well understood that they must sit quietly. Only the men would talk at the meeting.

But Mrs. Mott found that she could not stay silent. When a few men began to argue about what the group's aims should be, she stood up.

"I respectfully suggest," she said, "that we leave out the last two lines in Mr. Garrison's statement. Then it should satisfy all who are objecting."

A buzz of surprised voices arose as she took her seat again. None of those present had ever heard a woman speak at a public gathering. Some men thought that women should remain silent at home when important matters were discussed, and leave all decisions to men.

Still, what Mrs. Mott said made very good sense, and she spoke politely. The chairman rapped for order and then praised her.

6. "On to Motts'!"

Soon after the convention ended, Mrs. Mott helped to form the Philadelphia Female Anti-Slavery Society.

"In our own city, we women can do something that very much needs to be done," Mrs. Mott said.

So she and several Quaker friends visited the small group of black families living in Philadelphia. These families had won their freedom from slavery. However, they faced problems of every kind. The men had trouble finding jobs. Few schools welcomed their children.

Even so, they had not lost hope, for there were blacks like James Forten and his wife who helped them. Mr. Forten was a fine sailmaker and a natural leader. He owned his own business and served as the unofficial mayor of the black people of Philadelphia.

"We thank you for offering to help us," he told Mrs. Mott. "We like your plan of giving reading lessons to our boys and girls. But we would like to help too. Nobody can feel more deeply than we do about the need to free black people in the South. Will you let my wife join in your work?"

"That would please me very much," Mrs. Mott said.

For the next few years, the Female Anti-Slavery Society quietly did some useful work. A small school was started for black children. Black women were given sewing lessons. Food and medicine were provided for needy families.

Black women and white women worked together on these projects. Still, many Northerners did not agree with the antislavery movement. They thought that abolitionists, as antislavery people were called, were just stirring up trouble. "Black people are not the same as we are," they said. "They should not be treated as equals." Many felt that whites and blacks should not attend the same meetings.

In Philadelphia, in 1838, these feelings became stronger than ever.

A fine new meeting hall had just been built in the main part of the city. Several religious groups had given money to make this a center for antislavery programs. Mrs. Mott had invited women from antislavery societies in other cities to attend a meeting in Philadelphia. She hoped they would be able to plan new ways to work to end slavery.

On the day the meeting opened, a crowd of hoodlums gathered near the door of the hall. They shouted nasty words when white women and black women walked in together.

Mrs. Mott calmly rose to begin the meeting. "I hope," she said, "that no person will be alarmed by a little *appearance* of danger."

Yet the danger was real. That evening, after the

James and Lucretia Mott: devout Quakers and leaders in the antislavery movement.

women had left, a mob angrily set the new meeting hall on fire.

The hall was empty then, so no lives were lost. But the sight of the fine building going up in flames was not enough to satisfy the howling crowd. Someone remembered that Lucretia Mott was the leader of the women's group.

"On to Motts'!" The mob took up this terrible cry.

Half a mile away a few dozen men and women were sitting in the Motts' parlor talking about the meeting. Then came a loud knock at the front door. A breathless young man entered. He had never forgotten that Mrs. Mott had brought food and money to his family while his father was out of work. He quickly told her what was happening.

Mrs. Mott looked across the room at her husband. They knew each other so well that they needed no words. James Mott rose and went upstairs to get their young children. Then he took them to a neighbor's house for safety. A few minutes later he returned and calmly sat down again next to his wife. They were ready to face whatever might come.

However, the young man who had warned them was now hurrying back toward the center of town. When he met the mob he grabbed the elbow of one of the leaders. "The Motts' home is this way!" he cried. Purposely he pointed in the wrong direction. The trick worked.

When the hoodlums could not find the Motts' house, they began to drift away. Mr. and Mrs. Mott were safe. After the danger had passed, Lucretia spoke quietly to her husband. "I felt willing to suffer whatever the cause required," she said.

7. With Lizzie in London

Why had no police been sent to control the mob?

Many fair-minded people asked this question when they read about what had happened. Antislavery meetings were well protected from then on.

During the next two years, Mrs. Mott spent more and more time giving speeches about slavery. She spoke to Quakers, and she spoke to many other religious groups. "We all try to teach our children the difference between right and wrong," she told them. "Let us remember this difference ourselves. We must never forget that slavery is *wrong*!

"Slavery cannot be ended here," she went on, "until the majority of people in America realize that it is evil."

Mrs. Mott's hard work brought her an unexpected reward. In 1840 Garrison's American Anti-Slavery Society asked her to go to England. An antislavery meeting of people from all over the world was being planned in London. Four other American women were elected to attend the meeting too.

Mrs. Mott was now 47 years old. However, she felt as excited as a girl at the idea of making this trip. Her children were all old enough so she could safely leave them with relatives for a few months. Her husband was going with her. He would be a delegate too.

"We sail from New York on the fifth of May," Mrs. Mott wrote happily to one of her sisters. "I do so look forward to it."

The Great Anti-Slavery Meeting of 1841. In this artist's version of the London conference, women are sprinkled throughout the audience.

Soon after arriving in London, Mrs. Mott made a disturbing discovery. Although the American women had come a great distance, they were unwelcome at the meeting.

"This convention is not for women," Lucretia was told by an English abolitionist. "Women are unfit to attend meetings with men."

"It is surprising that *you* should think so," she told the abolitionist. "Those are the same words slave owners use. They say that black people are unfit to be with whites."

"We hope you will not insist on being seated at the meeting," said another man.

Lucretia and the other American ladies had talked this over. "We were elected by our antislavery societies to represent them," Lucretia told the Englishman politely. "We feel it is our duty to attend."

When the convention opened, James Mott and the other men took their places on the hall floor. Lucretia and the ladies were led to a balcony and seated behind a curtain. They were hidden from the view of the men delegates.

Lucretia shook her head. "This is too bad," she said.

"It surely is!" a dark-haired young woman cried.

She was the wife of a New York abolitionist who was attending the meeting. She had married him only a few weeks earlier and this trip was her honeymoon. As Miss Lizzie Cady, she had resented not only slavery, but also the unfair way women were treated. Her father was a judge, and she liked to read his law books. "Why can't girls become lawyers?" she kept asking him. "Why can't we go to college? What sense does it make to keep girls from using the brains God gave them?"

Now, as Mrs. Elizabeth Cady Stanton, she decided something had to be done.

"It's time," Lizzie Stanton sputtered to Mrs. Mott. "It's time some demand is made for new rights for women."

Mrs. Mott thought back to her own experiences as a teacher. She had been paid not a penny for her work, while men teachers earned fair salaries. She thought it most unjust for women to be kept from speaking at this abolitionist meeting.

"I agree with you, my dear," she said. "Let's discuss it after the meeting."

8. Busy Years

Before they left London, Mrs. Mott and Mrs. Stanton made a promise to each other. They would work on woman's rights as soon as possible. However, one thing after another kept them from doing this—including the Underground Railroad.

Ever since the early 1800s, some of Philadelphia's Quakers had been doing all they could to help runaway slaves. James and Lucretia Mott were proud to have their house serve as a station for these travelers from the South. Shortly after the Motts returned from Europe, they had an exciting few weeks.

First, they received word that a slave named Henry Brown had made up his mind to escape from the South. He had himself nailed in a box addressed to the Anti-Slavery Society in Philadelphia. It was loaded aboard a train in Virginia.

When that train finally arrived in the Philadelphia depot, James Mott and other members of the society were waiting. Workmen quickly lifted the box onto a wagon.

The men drove then to the office of the Anti-Slavery Society and carried the box safely indoors. One of them tapped gently on the wooden top.

"Are you all right?" he asked.

From inside the box a faint tap sounded. "All right, sir," a muffled voice said.

Until he got back his strength, Henry "Box" Brown stayed hidden in an upstairs room at the Motts'. Then James and Lucretia gave him food and money and directions to his next stop. Brown left Philadelphia on his way to freedom in Canada.

Soon after this Mrs. Mott went on a speaking trip. It took her through many northern states, then into

Mrs. Mott's escort walks with her through a threatening mob.

slave states. In churches and in meeting halls, she spoke fearlessly against slavery. Once her coach was hit with stones. At another meeting a riot broke out.

A clergyman at this meeting took her arm to lead her to safety. But she asked him to help some other women through the angry crowd.

"Who will take care of you?" the worried minister asked her.

"This man!" she said, putting her hand on the arm of one of the rioters. The man's mouth opened wide in surprise, but he did lead her through the mob. When some of his friends began teasing him, he said, "Well, she's a sensible woman. You can see that."

Wherever she spoke, people were impressed by Mrs. Mott. Many expected a woman speaker to be strange and unladylike. They were always surprised when they first saw her. In her Quaker bonnet and gray gown, she was the picture of a gentle woman. The tone of her voice was soft, and she never argued with her listeners. She tried to reason with them the way a good teacher would.

Mrs. Mott became so famous that she was invited to tea at the White House. There she tried to make President Tyler believe in the rightness of her cause.

"If all of your friends were as reasonable as you are, ma'am, I'd have more hope of solving this problem," he told her. The Virginia-born president was himself a slave owner.

Month after month, Mrs. Mott kept speaking at antislavery meetings in many cities. Year after year, she traveled wherever she thought she might do some good. Even those who did not agree with her about slavery gradually came to admire her.

In between meetings Mrs. Mott was busy with her family. In the summer of 1848 she visited a married sister who had moved to New York State. Her sister's home was near the village of Seneca Falls, where Elizabeth Cady Stanton now lived. So it happened that these two women finally met again.

9. The Right Time

"We must not wait any longer!" Lizzie Stanton said.

Mrs. Mott smiled. Her young friend had not grown more patient since becoming the mother of several lively little boys. The moment Lizzie heard that Lucretia Mott had arrived in the area, she left her boys with a neighbor and drove over to see her. Lizzie was demanding that they keep their promise to each other about working for woman's rights. They must hold a meeting at once.

"What good would it do to have a meeting in this country village?" Mrs. Mott asked gently.

"Some other ideas that have traveled far were thought of first right here!" Mrs. Stanton said.

Mrs. Mott had to admit this was true. "But is it a good plan to hold a meeting during the summer?" she asked. "Won't the wives of farmers be too busy to come?"

"We have waited too long already!"

Without another word Mrs. Stanton reached for a pen and paper. Then she wrote:

> WOMAN'S RIGHTS CONVENTION—A Convention to discuss the social, civil, and religious condition and rights of women, will be held in the Wesleyan Chapel, at Seneca Falls, N.Y., on Wednesday and Thursday, the 19th and 20th of July, current, starting at 10 o'clock, A.M. The public generally are invited to be present. . . . Lucretia Mott of Philadelphia . . . will address the Convention.

This was printed in the next issue of the local newspaper. Lucretia Mott was too modest to think that mention of her name would draw people from miles around. But nearly 300 women—and a good many men—did come to Seneca Falls.

Speaking with deep feeling, Mrs. Mott told them that the time had come for starting a movement for woman's rights. One of its main aims, she and Mrs.

Stanton had decided, was to gain equal educational opportunities for girls. Schools should teach girls the same subjects as boys, and colleges should open their doors to women. Women should have the right to work at other jobs besides just sewing and teaching. They should be able to be doctors, lawyers, and business leaders. They ought to be paid for their work at the same rate as men.

After almost every sentence a burst of clapping made Mrs. Mott wait for silence. When at last she finished, she called on Mrs. Elizabeth Cady Stanton.

Mrs. Stanton rose. She began to read sentences that had a familiar ring.

"We hold these truths to be self-evident," she read, "that all men *and women* are created equal."

The audience gasped at this bold change in the words of the Declaration of Independence. But that was only the beginning of Mrs. Stanton's boldness. She then read the rest of her own version of the famous words Thomas Jefferson had written in 1776.

Jefferson had listed the wrongs that led the thirteen colonies to break away from England. Mrs. Stanton gave one example after another of the wrongs suffered by the women of the United States. She pointed out that married women could not own property. If they did earn money, every penny belonged by law to their husbands.

Many changes had to come, she said. Unfair laws

had to be changed. Schools and businesses must begin to treat men and women equally. Most important of all, women must be given the right to vote.

"Why, Lizzie," Mrs. Mott broke in gently, "you will make us laughed at!"

To most people in 1848, giving women the right to vote was a daring idea. Mrs. Mott knew that many people would object. She feared the whole woman's rights program would become a joke.

"No!" said Lizzie Stanton. "Without the vote we will still be second-class citizens, even if we can go to college and earn equal money."

Mrs. Mott thought about this. "Perhaps you are right," she said finally.

After two days of talk, the people at the meeting agreed to work for woman's rights. A great new movement was on its way!

10. Progress?

"You were certainly right, Lucretia," Lizzie Stanton said cheerfully. She held up a newspaper that had just arrived by mail from Massachusetts.

On its front page was a story Mrs. Mott read with a sad little smile. If only men would take the women's plans seriously! Like dozens of other editors, this one was treating the woman's rights meeting in Seneca Falls as a great joke.

PROGRESS? was the headline above the article.

Then the story went on to poke fun at the idea of women wanting to change places with men. Wouldn't it be wonderful, the writer asked, if men took up washing dishes and mending clothes while their wives ran the country?

However, many women did not agree with the editors. After returning to Philadelphia, Mrs. Mott received dozens of letters. "Thank you for calling attention to our problems," she was told again and again.

It took Lizzie Stanton, though, to think of another idea. This one really made people talk about the woman's rights movement.

Mrs. Stanton had a cousin who had spent some time visiting Turkey. This cousin had brought back some trousers worn by women in that country. Lizzie at once decided this costume was much more practical than the long skirts American women wore.

So she sewed herself a pair of floppy trousers something like the Turkish ones, topped by a short skirt. Unfortunately, these did not fit her very well. Still, she wore them everywhere. She cheerfully ignored the teasing that followed. "It's such a relief not to have a skirt trailing in the mud," she wrote to Mrs. Mott.

However, Mrs. Stanton was not satisfied yet. She had a friend in Seneca Falls, a widow named Mrs.

Amelia Bloomer, who published a ladies' magazine. Mrs. Stanton asked her to print a picture of the Turkish trousers. Then supporters of woman's rights all over the United States could make them and enjoy freedom from long skirts. Soon these trousers came to be called "bloomers."

Within a few months, the whole country was laughing at women wearing bloomers.

Lucretia Mott never wore bloomers herself. She was too set in her ways to try a new style of dress. But she believed others should do as they wished.

Still, she was happy when Mrs. Stanton gave up wearing bloomers. She was also pleased when a young schoolteacher named Susan B. Anthony began to work for the cause of woman's rights.

Mrs. Mott knew that she herself was no longer able to do all she wanted to. Before breakfast every morning she still shelled peas or did other household jobs. She had company for dinner almost every day. But as her sixtieth birthday neared, she finally began to cut down on her work.

She could not refuse to go to the most important woman's rights meetings, of course. She still spoke at these gatherings. Her speeches were treated with respect by newspapers that otherwise poked fun at "hen conventions." Yet now she was glad to leave the planning of new programs to Susan Anthony.

In antislavery work, her speeches were no longer

as necessary as in the past. Public opinion had changed. "Now," Lucretia told her husband, "most people in the North agree that slavery is wrong." Lucretia knew that the antislavery work was being shared now by able men in politics. They were working to pass laws to stop slavery. Still, a terrible question remained.

How were the slaves to be freed without a war between the North and the South?

As a Quaker, Mrs. Mott had always hated fighting. "I am for peace," she said again and again. Word came one day that shooting had started in South Carolina. The nation was torn by a civil war. Mrs. Mott shut herself up in her room to pray.

She liked President Lincoln, but she could not speak in favor of the war.

By this time the Motts were living in the country outside Philadelphia. In 1857 James had decided that the time had come for him to retire from his business. So he bought a farm called Roadside, where tall trees shaded the front lawn. Here his wife enjoyed picking strawberries and making jam as she had done so long ago on Nantucket.

Here, too, she enjoyed one of the happiest days of her life. On a bright spring morning friends and relatives came to the farm. It was the fiftieth wedding anniversary of James and Lucretia Mott.

Their married daughters and their son all came

with their own families. With her grandchildren around her, Mrs. Mott sat holding one tiny great-grandchild on her lap.

She had always wanted very little for herself. So there was a problem about choosing a gift to give her on her golden wedding anniversary. But her dear ones solved it neatly—by presenting her with a pair of gold knitting needles.

"I shall remember this beautiful day whenever I use them," she said with tears of happiness in her eyes.

Another great day came in 1862 when President Lincoln signed the Emancipation Proclamation. Lucretia went to a joyful meeting of the Female Anti-Slavery Society. Their long years of work had not been wasted. The Southern slaves were free!

The war was still far from over. Even when she worked in her quiet garden, Mrs. Mott could not forget it. She worried about her nephews and the sons of friends who were in the midst of the fighting. And she grieved, because she still felt war was wrong.

11. "Yes, I Must Rest"

Mrs. Mott was joyful when the Civil War ended. She was pleased when black men were given the right to vote. But she was disappointed when women were not given the same right to vote. In letters to Elizabeth Stanton and Susan Anthony, she made no secret of her feelings.

Yet she herself felt a growing need for peace and quiet. Those in the fight for woman's rights, however, still thought of her as their leader. They often came to ask her advice. After one such visit she wrote in her diary:

"This equal rights movement is no play—but I cannot enter into it. Just hearing their talk made me ache all over, and be glad to come away and lie on the sofa. Yes, I must rest."

Mrs. Mott grew even weaker when she had to bear a great loss. Her beloved husband caught a cold five months before his eightieth birthday. He became seriously ill a few days later. Within the week, he died.

Lucretia Mott was then 74. It took her many months to get over her sorrow. Still, she surprised everyone by once again taking a lively interest in the world.

She even went on several trips by train to see her children and grandchildren. And she still showed the same independence that she always had had. When relatives wanted to take her home, she would say, "No, thank you, I don't need anyone. There is always somebody to help me in and out of the cars."

Mrs. Mott attended a public meeting from time to

time. When she was 85 she went to the thirtieth anniversary of the Seneca Falls meeting.

Frail as she was, she walked alone into the meeting hall. Frederick Douglass, the former slave who had become a great leader of the black citizens of America, was on the platform. He was speaking about the importance of getting equal rights for all citizens—black and white, male and female. He stopped speaking and walked forward to welcome Mrs. Mott.

Applause seemed to shake the very walls as he led her up onto the platform. With the gentle smile those present knew so well, Mrs. Mott tried to make herself heard above the cheering. "Thank you," she said. "Thank you all."

After she finished speaking, and with the same smile, she started walking alone down the steps toward the door. Speaking for that whole audience, Frederick Douglass called, "Good-bye, Lucretia!"

Back at home on her farm outside Philadelphia, cared for by loving friends, Mrs. Mott lived for two more years. She died in her sleep on November 11, 1880.

In many parts of the United States, solemn meetings were held. Quakers and people of other faiths wanted to pay their last respects to Lucretia Mott. "She was a rare person," many said. "She was never afraid to speak up against injustice."

Susan B. Anthony
Pioneer in Woman's Rights
by Helen Stone Peterson

Copyright © 1971 by Helen Stone Peterson

1. Susan Helps

Twelve-year-old Susan B. Anthony was setting the table for supper at the end of a lovely spring day in 1832. Her face lighted with a smile when she heard her father enter the house. Then his voice reached her as he spoke to her mother.

"Sally Ann who tends the spools at the mill is sick. I don't know anyone who can take her place."

Mr. Anthony was the managing partner of a large cloth mill in Battenville, New York. Six years earlier the Anthonys had moved to this village from Adams, Massachusetts, where Susan was born. Susan had often visited the mill and watched the machines weave cotton yarn into cloth. Now she ran to her father.

"I know Sally Ann's job and I'd like to take her place. Please let me, father."

A look of surprise came over Mr. Anthony's face. But he always encouraged his children to be independent, and he nodded his approval. "I believe it would be a useful experience," he said.

Mrs. Anthony gave a little gasp. "Don't you think

Susan is too young to work in the mill?" she protested gently.

Mr. Anthony smiled at Susan. "Your mother and I will discuss this and give you our decision."

Susan went back to setting the table. Just then her ten-year-old sister Hannah came into the room with a dish of yellow butter. When Hannah learned that Susan might work in the mill, she ran to tell her father that she too wanted the job.

The Anthonys were a big family. Susan and Hannah had a younger sister, Mary, a younger brother, Daniel, and an older sister, Guelma. Later another brother, Merritt, would complete the family circle.

At supper Mr. Anthony talked to Susan and Hannah. "Your mother has agreed to let one of you tend the spools. You will draw straws for the job, and the winner must divide the wages with the loser."

Susan drew the longest straw—and won. For the next two weeks she worked in the mill from six o'clock in the morning until six at night. Then she spent all her share of the earnings to buy six blue china cups and saucers. She gave this present to her mother.

"Thank you, my dear." Mrs. Anthony spoke quietly as she always did, but a pleased smile brightened her tired face and warmed Susan's heart.

Mrs. Anthony toiled from dawn to dark, and her daughters cheerfully assisted her. Susan, taking tiny stitches, skillfully mended stockings and hemmed towels. She baked golden loaves of bread and cooked delicious puddings.

In the spring of 1832 food had to be prepared in larger quantities than usual, for Mr. Anthony's brickmakers were taking their meals with the family. Susan's father had hired these men to make bricks for the new home he was building. The house the family now lived in was only one and a half stories high. The new house would be much bigger.

"We will have fifteen rooms and four fireplaces," Mr. Anthony told his family. With great pleasure he described the handsome curving stairway he planned for the entrance hall.

"Oh, it will be a beautiful home," exclaimed Susan, her eyes sparkling.

As soon as the Anthonys were settled in their new home, they invited their friends and relatives to visit them. They came, calling out good wishes to the family and filling the fine rooms with laughter. Happily Susan and her sisters poured lemonade and passed plates of doughnuts and gingerbread.

Mr. Anthony was growing wealthy. He now owned a second cloth mill, a small one, in Hardscrabble, a few miles away. In addition, he and his partner had built some tenant houses and a store in Battenville. Over the store Mr. Anthony had started a private school because he wanted his children to be taught by better teachers than those at the village school. Other children were invited to attend.

Soon Mr. Anthony moved his school to a large, attractive room in the new house. This was the first Battenville classroom in which each pupil had a separate seat. Though the seats were only stools without backs, the children were delighted not to be crowded onto the usual benches.

Susan took a fancy to Mary Perkins who came there to teach for a while. Miss Perkins supplied the pupils with books that had pictures. Susan, who had never seen such beautiful schoolbooks before, eagerly turned the pages.

When the children grew tired of bending over their books, Miss Perkins led them in physical exercises. The pupils enjoyed this new break in the school day and did all of the exercises with vigor.

The year Susan was fifteen, she became the teacher for small children who attended the school during the summer months. She taught there again the following summer. Then, shortly after her seventeenth birthday in February 1837, Susan left home for the first time. She went to teach the children of a family in a neighboring village.

That fall Susan was ready to go much farther

from home. Mr. Anthony wanted his daughters, as well as his sons, to have more education than was available to them in his school. At this time the only college in the country that would admit women was Oberlin, in Ohio, but there were boarding schools where girls could take some advanced courses. Susan's sister Guelma was starting her second year in a boarding school near Philadelphia. In November 1837 Susan went there too.

This school was run by a Quaker lady. It was natural that Mr. Anthony had chosen a Quaker school, for he and his children were Quakers. Mrs. Anthony was not, though she regularly attended Quaker meetings with her family.

Susan expected to be a student at the school for two years. But after she had been there only six months, her father arrived one day with bad news.

"Our business is ruined, and our large mill has failed," Mr. Anthony told his daughters.

Susan, seeing the despair on her father's face, could hardly keep from weeping. She knew that other cloth mills were failing. The nation was suffering the worst financial crash in its history.

"What are you going to do?" asked Susan brokenly.

"I don't know," her father replied.

"Oh, I shall help him," Susan vowed.

The girls returned home with their father. Before long, some men to whom Mr. Anthony owed money claimed the beautiful house. Everything in it was put up for sale—even Mr. and Mrs. Anthony's eyeglasses.

"What a nightmare for my father and mother," thought Susan.

To her joy a kind uncle arrived. He bought the things the family wanted most to keep and gave them back to the Anthonys.

The family then moved to Hardscrabble, later called Center Falls. Mr. Anthony still owned the small cloth mill there, though it was heavily in debt. Now he hoped to build up the mill and make it successful.

Susan started to teach again and gave her father every dollar she could spare. One year she taught in the local village school. Other years she taught in schools farther away. At vacation time she hurried home, for she loved to be with her family.

Susan and her sisters had fun with other young people in their neighborhood. On summer days, laughing and talking, they climbed into buggies and drove off to picnics. In the winter they went sleigh riding over the snowy roads, with sleigh bells jingling. The young men placed thick heated planks under the girls' feet to keep them warm.

More than one man asked Susan to marry him, but there was no one for whom she really cared enough. "I would only become a household drudge,"

Susan told herself, "or maybe a doll." She chuckled at that thought.

As the years went by, Susan's father continued to work hard. Still, he could not make a success of his small cloth mill. He thought he might do better as a farmer, so he and his wife decided to move to a farm in Rochester, New York.

Guelma and Hannah did not go with the family, since both were now married and had their own homes close to Center Falls. Daniel, working nearby, chose to stay at his job. But on a cold November day in 1845, Susan and the rest of her family boarded a barge at the eastern end of the Erie Canal. The horses on the towpath pulled, the barge jerked forward, and the Anthonys were on their way to Rochester.

2. "Yah! Yah! Bloomer!"

Susan helped her family settle into their farmhouse. Then in the spring she left to teach the girls at Canajoharie Academy in eastern New York.

Susan was now making as much money as a woman teacher could make. Yet she was paid only a fraction of the salary a man received for the same work. A woman teacher was always paid less, simply because she was a woman. Susan had long resented this inequality.

After three years at the academy, Susan resigned. "I will not spend the rest of my life teaching school," she decided. "But what shall I do?" To this question Susan did not yet know the answer.

She went back to her family's home. Her father, having found the farm too small to provide a living, was starting in the insurance business. To give him more time for building up his new business, Susan took over the management of the farm.

One day her father drove her in his buggy to call on his new friend Frederick Douglass, the former black slave, who lived in Rochester. Mr. Douglass was publishing a newspaper in which he kept demanding immediate freedom for the millions of black slaves in the South. Many Northerners hated him. Businessmen, who were making money by trading with Southerners, did not want trouble stirred up. There were even preachers who said that blacks were born to serve white people.

But the Anthonys believed it was wicked to hold men as property. Susan found that she had the same views on slavery as Frederick Douglass. From their first meeting, she and the black leader were friends.

The Douglass family often spent lively Sundays at the Anthony farmhouse. "Mr. Douglass always brought along his violin," Susan remembered. "He liked to play it and sing, and we were happy listening to him."

When antislavery lecturers were in that part of the state, Mr. Anthony also invited them to spend Sunday at the farm. Among these lecturers were a few women. As they talked in the Anthony home or spoke in a meeting hall, Susan listened with admiration. Usually women were not permitted to say anything before an audience, but now a few courageous ones were speaking out against slavery.

"Shame on you women! Your place is clearly in the home," cried ministers.

Newspapermen wrote angrily, "Women do not belong in public life."

Susan became so interested in antislavery lectures that she sometimes went out of town to hear them. In May 1851 Susan, now 31, went to an antislavery meeting in Seneca Falls near Rochester. As she and a friend walked along a street of that village, they unexpectedly met Elizabeth Cady Stanton. The friend introduced Susan to Mrs. Stanton.

"I have longed to meet you," said Susan, a warm smile sweeping over her rather plain face. Mrs. Stanton, a brilliant woman, was short and plump, with twinkling eyes and beautiful curly hair.

Susan knew that here at Seneca Falls in 1848, Mrs. Stanton and her Quaker friend Lucretia Mott had called the world's first convention for woman's rights. The women had drawn up a document protesting that they were being treated as if they were inferior to men. Mrs. Stanton had dared to go so far as to demand the right to vote, or suffrage, for women.

Before leaving Seneca Falls Susan called on Mrs. Stanton, and they had a long talk. "Remember the injustices to women as well as to the slaves," urged Mrs. Stanton. "A husband, no matter how worthless, is sole guardian of his children and can even give them away in his will. Every penny that a wife earns belongs to her husband." Mrs. Stanton went on to explain more injustices suffered by women.

"I tell you," she exclaimed, "there is mighty work to be done to lift woman to her proper place."

"She will be in her proper place when she has equal rights with men," answered Susan thoughtfully. "I believe in equal rights for all regardless of sex or color."

Mrs. Stanton, nodding in agreement, added firmly, "The most important right is the vote. When we have the right to vote, we can change laws." After Susan returned to Rochester, she began to think hard about the importance of the right to vote.

A few weeks later she was invited back to Seneca Falls by Mrs. Stanton. This time Susan met Lucy Stone, the eloquent speaker from Massachusetts. Since Mrs. Stanton was busy raising a large family, Lucy Stone became the leader in organizing a national convention every year.

"It is wrong that we women are governed by laws in which we have no voice," Lucy said to Susan as they sat together in Mrs. Stanton's parlor. "We must fight for the right to vote." Though Lucy was very small, weighing only about 100 pounds, she was full of courage, and her bright eyes flashed with determination.

The next year Susan attended her first woman's rights convention. Soon she reached an important decision. "What shall I do?" she had asked herself when she gave up teaching. At last she knew the answer to this question.

"I shall work for equal rights for all," she decided, "and my goal will be to win for women the right to vote." Susan felt confident that she would find a way to support herself. She had some savings and she had the backing of her father, who agreed with her decision wholeheartedly.

Now Susan took an unusual step. She put on the comfortable bloomer costume that had been designed by Elizabeth Miller, a cousin of Mrs. Stanton. It consisted of a loose dress that came a little below the knees and trousers that were gathered at the ankles. In this outfit women were no longer tightly laced at the waist, nor weighed down with pounds of long petticoats. The costume was named after Amelia Bloomer, who publicized it in a paper she edited at Seneca Falls.

Amelia Bloomer (left) in her original costume, designed to free women from petticoats. A later version of the "bloomer" is seen at the right.

"Yah! Yah! Bloomer!" Boys made fun of Susan when she walked along the street. They jeered at all women who appeared in the new style.

Once Susan and Lucy Stone wore their bloomers to New York City where they attended a meeting. As they walked away from the meeting, they noticed that they were being pursued by a group of boys. Susan and Lucy moved quickly, but the boys moved even faster. They completely surrounded the two women and held them prisoner. Lots of people stopped to enjoy the sight, while the boys shouted:

> *Gibbery, gibbery gab*
> *The women had a confab*
> *And demanded the rights*
> *To wear the tights*
> *Gibbery, gibbery gab.*

Susan and Lucy stood facing each other, helpless. Just then, a man who knew them both pushed through the crowd. With the aid of a policeman, he led the women to his carriage.

Susan continued to wear the bloomer costume for a while, but then gave it up.

"The costume attracted too much unfavorable attention," Susan told friends. "It was hurting the woman's rights movement." With a laugh she added, "I hope our other reforms will be more successful."

3. "Ladies Always Have the Best Places"

Most newspapers were hostile to the woman's rights movement. "What are the rights which women seek?" scoffed the New York *Sun*. "The right to do wrong!"

Reporters ridiculed the women's meetings, calling them "tomfoolery conventions." They made fun of the speeches there. "Gabble," wrote reporters. "Silly rant."

"The whole world is against us," cried many women reformers. "How can we begin changing the status of women?"

"We can demand new laws from our state legislatures," proposed Susan, who had assumed the leadership in New York.

She drew up a petition that requested new laws to bring three reforms for women: the right to vote, the right of married women to control their earnings, and the right to have equal guardianship of their children. At this time the establishment of voting rights, along with these other rights, was left to the individual states.

To circulate the petition throughout New York, Susan enlisted women who wanted these changes. All the women, like Susan, were volunteer workers in different parts of the state. Susan herself canvassed the Rochester area.

In the cold winter of 1854, Susan tramped through the snow from house to house and asked for signatures on the petition. Many a housewife slammed the door in her face, snapping, "I have all the rights I want. Thank heaven, I have a husband to look after me."

Yet in two months the faithful workers collected a total of 10,000 signatures. After Susan presented the signed petition to the legislature in Albany, Mrs. Stanton was allowed to address the lawmakers. She was the first woman to speak before the legislature. With pride Susan listened to her friend's scholarly plea for woman's rights. But the legislature refused to enact the requested laws.

"We shall keep coming back here until we get positive action," Susan warned the lawmakers.

The next year Susan traveled alone from one isolated village to another throughout the state. She lectured on woman's rights and asked for more signatures on the petition. This tour took courage.

So unpopular was the women's movement that in one town Susan was denied the use of the meeting halls. The hotel owner came to her rescue and turned his dining room into a meeting room. In some towns there was no way for Susan to announce her lecture except by notices that she handed out or nailed up in conspicuous spots.

To cover her expenses, she charged an admission fee of 25¢ to the meetings. In Canandaigua thirteen-year-old Caroline Richards went to hear Susan. This is what the schoolgirl wrote in her diary:

> Susan B. Anthony . . . talked very plainly about our rights and how we ought to stand up for them, and said the world would never go right until

> the women had just as much right to vote and rule as the men. . . . I could not make grandmother agree with her at all and she said we might better all of us stayed at home.

At the end of her tour in 1855, Susan presented the petition to the legislature, but the lawmakers still did nothing. She patiently went back to lecturing and enrolling more names. In 1856, after she delivered the petition to the legislature, a committee wrote a report. As the chairman read it to the lawmakers, they burst into laughter.

> . . . The ladies always have the best places and choicest tidbit at the table. They have the best seats in the [railroad] cars, carriages, and sleighs; the warmest place in winter and the coolest in summer. . . . If there is any inequality . . . the gentlemen are the sufferers.

"How dare they make fun of all our hard work!" flared Susan, reading the story in the Albany *Register*. But her indignation quickly passed, leaving room only for her determination to persist in bringing pressure on the lawmakers.

LEADERS IN THE WOMAN'S RIGHTS MOVEMENT OF THE 1880s.

Susan B. Anthony

Elizabeth Cady Stanton

Lucy Stone

Among other things, Susan took the initiative in arranging a woman's rights convention at Albany each year while the legislature was in session. Women came from every corner of the state, bringing the lawmakers more signatures.

In 1860 the legislature finally acted. Women did not get the right to vote. But the lawmakers passed a bill that gave to married women the control of their earnings and equal guardianship of their children.

"We have won a great victory!" Susan joyfully told her co-workers. Woman's rights legislation, like that enacted in New York, spread from state to state.

4. Free the Slaves

By this time Susan was also working for the American Anti-Slavery Society at a salary of ten dollars a week. The society, recognizing her leadership ability, had asked Susan to take charge of its work in New York State.

"I welcome this opportunity," Susan told her family. Like all the Anthonys she regarded slavery as evil, and she wanted to do something about it.

Slavery was becoming a burning national issue. Americans were divided as to whether it should be extended to the new states entering the Union. Only a minority took the position of the Anti-Slavery Society, which demanded: "Free the slaves now!"

Susan threw herself into the work of planning schedules for the society's lecturers, who traveled in groups throughout the state. She always accompanied one of the groups. While traveling with an able black man and his sister, Susan ran into bitter racial hate. In some communities no hotel or boardinghouse would take in her two black friends.

"What lack of Christianity!" protested Susan. Blazing with anger, she would hunt until she found a private home where they could stay.

Susan knew that in many churches black families had to sit in pews apart from white people. Moreover, most of the state's public schools had separate classes for black children. In her lectures Susan lashed out at this discrimination.

"Here in the North Negroes are barred from many hotels, restaurants, churches, and schools."

"What do you want us to do with the blacks?" a hostile listener would ask.

Susan was always quick with her reply. "Treat the Negroes with equality and justice."

Flaming with fierce indignation over school segregation, Susan took time to attend a state teachers' convention where she introduced a long resolution that started this way: "Resolved: that the exclusion of colored youth from our public schools, academies, colleges, and universities is the result of wicked prejudice. . . ."

The convention broke into an uproar, and the teachers refused to approve the resolution. Instead, they adopted this statement: "The colored children of the state should enjoy equal advantages of education with the white."

In the winter of 1861, before the inauguration of the new president, Abe Lincoln, Susan met a group of antislavery speakers in western New York where they began a tour across the state. They found excitement at a high pitch, for southern states were seceding. Many Northerners truly were horrified at this breaking up of the Union.

Some of them thundered, "Don't let antislavery speakers be heard! Their agitation is the cause of all our troubles."

In Buffalo where Susan and the group were to speak, rioters rushed into the hall. They shouted, stamped, and whistled, so that it was impossible for the lecturers to be heard.

Attacks on the antislavery movement spread elsewhere. At Port Byron, where Susan was presiding over a meeting, rowdies threw a large quantity of red pepper on the hot stove in the hall. Everyone fled from the suffocating fumes. In Syracuse, as soon as Susan and the other speakers stepped onto the platform, rotten eggs were thrown at them. Rough-looking men with pistols in their pockets surged toward the platform, shouting, "Throw them out!"

Friends escorted the group quickly through a rear door. That night a hideous effigy labeled SUSAN B. ANTHONY was burned in the public square, while a drunken crowd screamed.

"Call off the rest of your meetings," a friend pleaded with Susan. "The danger of violence is too great."

"No," replied Susan, her courage unwavering. "Freedom of speech is one of our most important American rights, and it's our duty to uphold it."

Yet only in Albany, the last stop on the tour, were the brave lecturers heard. There the mayor placed policemen in the audience, and he himself sat on the speakers' platform with a loaded gun across his knee.

In April cannons at Charleston, South Carolina, fired on Fort Sumter, occupied by Union soldiers. The tragic Civil War had begun.

5. Amendments to the Constitution

Susan's beloved father died in November 1862 after a brief illness. For weeks Susan was desolate. Then she pulled herself together. "I will go forward," she resolved, knowing this is what her father would have wanted. He had always encouraged her to keep working toward equal rights for all.

Susan went to visit the Stantons in New York City, where they now lived. With the outbreak of the

Civil War, the drive for woman's rights had come to a halt. Instead, women were making bandages for the wounded, nursing in hospitals, and working in factories and on farms in place of men who had gone to war.

"What can we do for our country?" Susan and Mrs. Stanton asked each other.

They soon found the answer. The Emancipation Proclamation, recently issued by President Lincoln, had freed the slaves in the rebellious states. But, if slavery was to be forever prohibited in the United States, emancipation must be written into the Constitution by means of an amendment. Charles Sumner, the Republican senator from Massachusetts, was pressing for this amendment, but a majority of the members of Congress were not ready to vote for it. They had to be convinced that public opinion supported the amendment.

Susan and Mrs. Stanton organized the Women's National Loyal League, which would circulate petitions demanding that Congress pass the amendment. Susan became the league's paid worker, putting in long hours at her tiny office in New York.

"I go to a restaurant nearby for lunch," she wrote to her mother in the summer of 1863. "I always take strawberries with two tea rusks."

Susan mailed petitions to women from Maine to California. As signed petitions flowed back to her office, Mrs. Stanton's sons rolled them into huge bundles. Then they wrapped the bundles in yellow paper and tied them with red tape. On February 9, 1864, two strong men carried the bundles into the Senate and placed them on Senator Sumner's desk.

"You are doing a noble work," the senator wrote to the league. "Send on the petitions as fast as received."

By summer the league had sent petitions bearing almost 400,000 signatures, the largest number of names that had ever been collected in the United States for a single objective. This achievement helped convince Congress that public opinion supported the Thirteenth Amendment, which was now moving toward passage. The league disbanded.

The next year Susan made a long visit to her brothers Daniel and Merritt in Kansas where they now lived. Here, soon after the end of the war, Susan read in a newspaper the text of the proposed Fourteenth Amendment. It would extend citizenship and the vote to blacks. But Susan was shocked to see the word "male" used three times to define voters. That word had never before appeared in the Constitution.

"If the word 'male' is written into the Constitution, it will be a new roadblock between women and the vote," thought Susan in alarm. "Now is the time for both Negroes and women to get the vote."

Ending her visit at once, Susan hastened to New York. She found Mrs. Stanton half frantic with concern over the possible introduction of the word "male" into the Constitution.

Together they wrote a petition that demanded the vote for women. Then they mailed copies to workers in the women's movement, along with letters requesting that the petition be signed and sent to Congress. To Susan's dismay, Senator Sumner was not pleased with the avalanche of petitions.

"These petitions are untimely and inopportune," he told the Senate. The Republican party, which was in power, refused to champion the vote for women. Intent on getting the votes of black men in the South, Republicans were determined to fight only for male black suffrage.

Confidently Susan turned for support to the antislavery men by whose side women had worked long and hard to free the slaves. She was bitterly disappointed when these men now turned their backs on woman suffrage. Wendell Phillips, president of the Anti-Slavery Society, said, "This is the Negro's hour. Do not clog his way."

The Fourteenth Amendment became part of the Constitution. It was followed by the Fifteenth Amendment that further protected the blacks' right to vote. Susan thought about the future of the black in America, and she spoke gravely to Mrs. Stanton.

"The white people must be educated to share their privileges with the blacks. And little children must be taught about human rights with the same exactness they are now taught the multiplication table. It is far more important for them to understand that all men are created equal, than to know that two times two equals four."

Susan's kind, honest face took on a look of iron determination. "As for me, my work will not be done until the power of the ballot is in the hands of all women—black and white."

6. Campaigning in Kansas

In 1867 Kansas submitted to voters an amendment to the state constitution that would give the ballot to women. For the first time in the United States, woman suffrage was being put to the vote.

"Send your strongest speakers to canvass this state for the amendment," a Republican state senator wrote to Susan. He knew that she was a leader in the suffrage movement.

"How I would rejoice to have one state where women might cast their ballots as naturally as their husbands do," thought Susan, filled with hope.

She persuaded Lucy Stone to spend the spring months in Kansas, speaking for the amendment. By September Susan and Mrs. Stanton had gone to the state. Susan, establishing headquarters in Lawrence, was the campaign manager.

Mrs. Stanton started over the prairie trails on a long, hard speaking tour. The strong mules pulling her carriage wore themselves out and had to be replaced by Indian ponies.

Three members of the well-known Hutchinson family, the most popular singing group in the North, came to help. They traveled through Kansas in their own carriage, drawn by two white horses.

With them Susan sent Reverend Olympia Brown, a talented woman minister who had come all the way from New England to help. Reverend Brown would speak briefly at meetings, urging passage of the amendment. Then the Hutchinsons would start singing:

> *Who votes for woman suffrage now*
> *Will add new laurels to his brow.*

Though many people did their very best for the campaign, Susan saw that the amendment was in great danger. She had counted on the Republican party to sponsor it. But the party in Kansas was split, and the most powerful group now actively opposed giving the ballot to women.

Susan was heartsick. "Where can we get support?" she asked herself.

Suddenly a telegram arrived from wealthy George Francis Train who offered to come and win Democratic votes for the amendment. Susan consulted Mrs. Stanton and other workers. All knew that Mr. Train was eccentric, for he often said and did absurd things. But they knew also that they needed help desperately. They accepted his offer.

Lucy Stone denounced Susan and Mrs. Stanton for linking George Train's name to the cause. She and some other people in the East considered him "crackbrained."

Nevertheless, Susan accompanied Mr. Train on his campaign through Kansas. On the platform he was a showman, wearing lavender kid gloves and shiny patent leather boots.

One day, while driving to a meeting, Mr. Train asked Susan, "Why don't you women have your own newspaper?"

"Lack of money," replied Susan grimly. She had longed to have a paper through which she could educate public opinion on woman's right to vote.

"Well, I will give you the money," said Mr. Train. Susan did not believe he was serious. But that evening, as soon as Mr. Train stepped onto the platform, he made an announcement:

"When Miss Anthony gets back to New York City, she is going to start a woman suffrage paper. It will be called the *Revolution*. She will be the owner." He named Mrs. Stanton as one editor and Parker Pillsbury, a loyal friend of both women, as the second editor.

Meanwhile, on election day the amendment that would have given the ballot to women in Kansas was defeated, receiving 9,000 votes out of a total of 30,000. However, Susan was not discouraged. She told Mrs. Stanton, "Nine thousand forward-looking men voted for woman suffrage. I believe our drive is gaining."

7. *The Revolution*

The first issue of the *Revolution* was on the newsstands in New York City on January 8, 1868. It was a handsome paper, a little smaller than today's tabloids. With pride Susan mailed 10,000 copies across the land.

"Let women demand the right to vote in thunder terms," urged the *Revolution*.

Soon a crushing burden fell upon Susan. Assuring her that he would send money for the paper, Mr. Train departed for Great Britain. There he spoke out for Irishmen who wanted their country freed from Great Britain. The British government arrested Mr. Train and sentenced him to prison. After a short time no more funds came for the *Revolution*.

Susan began to borrow money to keep the weekly

paper going. She worked day and night to secure subscriptions for it. Her efforts took her to Washington, D.C. She even went to the White House to ask President Andrew Johnson to add his name to the paper's subscription list. The *Revolution* carried an account of her visit there:

"I waited two hours in the anteroom among huge half-bushel-measure spittoons and terrible filth . . . where the smell of tobacco . . . was powerful," reported Susan.

When Susan did at last see the president, he said that he didn't want the paper. "I have a thousand such applications every day," he explained wearily.

"Mr. President, you are mistaken. You never had an application like this in your life," replied Susan bluntly. She talked about woman's right to the ballot and warned that her paper would keep hammering away until women got their rights.

"That brought him to his pocketbook," reported Susan. "He signed his name, Andrew Johnson, with a bold hand, as much as to say, 'Anything to get rid of this woman.'"

While Susan went about the business of publishing her paper, she became concerned over the problems of working women. Having entered the labor market during the Civil War, women were working in increasing numbers. Susan invited them to a meeting in the office of the *Revolution*.

They came—careworn seamstresses, milliners, clerks, factory workers, and typesetters. All these workers put in ten to fourteen hours a day and some of them earned as little as four dollars a week.

"Women, listen to me," urged Susan. "You must not work for these starving wages any longer. Have a spirit of independence!"

She helped them organize a Working Women's Association that aimed at improving conditions. It was deeply satisfying to Susan when the typesetters, with her aid, went on to organize their own union. This was one of the first women's unions in the United States.

"Stick to this union," advised Susan earnestly. "Together say 'Equal pay for equal work.'"

The *Revolution* fearlessly reported the problems of working women and news of their organization. But this coverage stirred up criticism of the paper because the subject was unpopular with conservative people.

The *Revolution* called for many reforms, including more liberal divorce laws. Since there was opposition to divorce for any reason, the paper's liberal ideas again offended conservative people. Lucy Stone was outraged that the question was brought up in a suffragists' paper.

In May 1869 Susan and Mrs. Stanton decided that the time had come to have a new, nationwide organ-

A meeting of the National Woman Suffrage Association

ization with the sole purpose of winning the vote for women. Under their leadership the National Woman Suffrage Association was formed.

Lucy Stone and her followers in New England did not join. For them the *Revolution* was too liberal, and they had never forgiven Susan and Mrs. Stanton for associating with Mr. Train. In November 1869 Lucy led in founding a rival organization, the American Woman Suffrage Association.

On January 8, 1870, exactly two years after the first issue of the *Revolution*, Lucy and her friends began publishing a suffrage paper, known as the *Woman's Journal*. It had financial backing and conservative editors.

The field was not large enough to support two papers, and the *Revolution* lost out. Susan loved her paper. When she had to give it up in May 1870, her heart almost broke.

"It was like signing my own death warrant," Susan wrote in her diary with anguish.

She personally assumed the *Revolution*'s staggering debt of $10,000. Bravely Susan promised, "I will work with might and main to pay every dollar of this honest debt."

8. Susan Votes

After Susan gave up the *Revolution*, she went to work as a lecturer.

By this time women who were good speakers were in great demand. Many people preferred to go to an auditorium to listen to an interesting speaker rather than stay at home and read. All over the country large audiences turned out to hear Susan plead for woman's right to vote.

But many newspapers called her a mischief-maker. And they sneered at her appearance, describing her as an angular, sour old maid. "If all woman's righters look like that, the theory will lose ground . . . ," wrote the Detroit *Free Press* in an insulting article.

Bearing herself with dignity, Susan paid no attention to the jibes. Many people in her audiences liked Susan's appearance. "She is an intelligent-looking woman," they remarked. They saw too that she was tastefully dressed. On the platform Susan always wore a dark silk gown with a collar of white lace.

She earned good fees for her lectures. By 1872 she had reduced the debt of the *Revolution* by several thousand dollars.

Susan was now considering woman suffrage from a new angle. Some lawyers claimed that women who were citizens of the United States already had the right to vote under the Fourteenth Amendment. These lawyers said, "The vote is a privilege of citizenship."

"I shall test this possibility," decided Susan as the national election of 1872 drew close.

On November 1 she was in Rochester, where her sisters Guelma and Hannah now lived with their families. Susan asked them and her sister Mary to go with her to register as voters. At the shoemaker's shop, which was the place for registering, the four sisters asked the election inspectors to enroll them.

"What do you say?" one inspector asked another.

"I say it's unlawful," came the reply.

"And I say it is your duty!" declared Susan. After an hour-long discussion with the inspectors, she persuaded them to register her as well as her three sisters. Then Susan rushed to the homes of friends in her part of the city, urging all the women to register.

On election day, November 5, 1872, Susan triumphantly entered her polling place and voted. Fourteen other women also voted there.

Two weeks later a United States marshal rang Susan's doorbell. "I have a warrant for your arrest," he told Susan. "You are charged with voting without a lawful right."

Susan's trial opened on June 17, 1873, in a crowded courtroom at Canandaigua, New York. Susan studied the prim-looking judge, Ward Hunt, and the all-male jury. "It's a man's world here," she thought. "Can a woman get justice?"

Susan's lawyer, Mr. Henry Selden of Rochester, made a masterly presentation of her case. Then the district attorney argued for the government.

When he finished, Susan was shocked to see Judge Hunt pull from his pocket a paper he had written before hearing the evidence. Now he read it aloud. In this prepared opinion the judge held that the question was one of law, and he directed the jury to find Susan guilty.

Mr. Selden jumped to his feet. "I ask your Honor to submit this case to the jury."

Ignoring Mr. Selden, the judge ordered the clerk to record the verdict. "Gentlemen of the jury," recited the clerk, ". . . you say you find the defendant guilty. . . ."

The jurors looked dazed. They had not said a single word.

Again Mr. Selden jumped to his feet. "Poll the jury!"

"No," ruled the high-handed judge. And to the jury he said, "Gentlemen of the jury, you are discharged."

The next day Susan returned to the courtroom for sentencing. Judge Hunt ordered her to stand up and then asked, "Have you anything to say?"

"Yes, your Honor, I have many things to say," retorted Susan. "You have trampled underfoot every vital principle of our government. . . ."

The judge tried to hush her, asserting that he could not listen to her arguments any longer.

Susan persisted in listing the rights that had been denied to her: "Your denial of my citizen's right to vote . . . , the denial of my right to a trial by a jury. . . ."

"Sit down!" ordered the judge.

But Susan continued until she finished what she wanted to say about injustices. Then she sat down.

"Stand up!" ordered the judge. He pronounced her sentence, a fine of one hundred dollars. She would also have to pay the cost of the trial.

"Your Honor, I shall never pay a dollar of your unjust penalty," declared Susan. And she never did.

But the judge did not order her to prison for

failure to pay. He knew that if Susan were imprisoned, she could appeal to a higher court. The government dropped its case against the other women who had voted with Susan.

Another test case, however, was traveling up through the courts. In 1875 the Supreme Court handed down the decision that women could not vote under the Fourteenth Amendment.

"Doesn't this decision discourage you?" a reporter asked Susan.

"Never!" she shot back. "I shall work without ceasing for an amendment that gives the ballot to women."

9. The Nation's Hundredth Birthday

Susan continued her strenuous lecture tours back and forth across the country. No one ever heard her complain, but she looked tired and worn.

At last there came a wonderful day. On May 1, 1876, Susan's blue eyes were shining as she wrote in her diary: "I have paid the last dollar of the *Revolution* debt!"

Later in the month Susan hurried to bustling Philadelphia. It was America's centennial year, the hundredth birthday of the founding of the nation in 1776. In celebration a huge exposition was to be held at Philadelphia during the summer. Susan saw that the exposition offered women a golden opportunity to focus attention on their right to vote and on the need for a woman suffrage amendment to the Constitution.

Mrs. Stanton and other leaders in the National Woman Suffrage Association joined Susan in Philadelphia. Together the leaders wrote a Declaration of Rights for Women. Susan asked permission to present this declaration at the large meeting planned for the Fourth of July in Independence Square.

"No," replied General Joseph Hawley, chairman of the centennial commission. "We propose to celebrate what we have done in the last hundred years, not what we have failed to do."

Then these suffrage leaders decided that it would be fitting for a woman from each state to sit on the big platform, alongside all the men who would sit there. They asked for seats for the women.

"Impossible!" replied General Hawley. "The platform is already crowded."

At the denial of these requests, Susan and her co-workers rebelled. "We *shall* leave one bright remembrance for the women of the next centennial," they vowed. "The daughters of 1976 will know that the women of 1876 asserted their right to equality."

They made plans for confrontation and action.

Susan succeeded in obtaining several admission

tickets to the platform. On the Fourth of July she and three co-workers took seats there. They listened while a man read the Declaration of Independence. When he was finished, the audience rose.

"Now!" Susan directed her followers.

The women marched forward. Thrusting a rolled parchment scroll into the hands of the presiding official, Susan said, "I present to you a Declaration of Rights from the women citizens of the United States."

The official's face went white, but he bowed and said nothing.

The women walked out of the meeting, handing to the left and right copies of their declaration. Men stretched out their hands for the paper. Others, farther away, stood on their seats and shouted that they wanted copies.

"Order!" boomed General Hawley. The general, having been busy with some details, had missed the beginning of this scene. But now his voice kept booming: "Order! Order!"

After the centennial, Susan embarked on a campaign to compel congressional action on a woman suffrage amendment. She urged the American Woman Suffrage Association to join in this effort. Its leaders, though, preferred to work for the vote in individual states, as Lucy Stone, Susan, and Mrs. Stanton had done in Kansas. The National

Susan B. Anthony at her desk, surrounded by the mementos of a lifelong battle for woman's rights.

Association cooperated in state campaigns, but it insisted that the best way of winning suffrage was by an amendment to the Constitution.

The National Association, having grown in the seven years since its origin, now had members across the nation. Susan asked them to collect signatures on petitions for the proposed amendment. The women brought the petitions to Washington, D.C., when they came for their convention in January 1877.

One afternoon, just as members of the House of Representatives were finishing their day's work, Susan led a group of women into their chamber. To each representative the women handed petitions from his own state.

The next day Susan led the group to the Senate. After the women presented their petitions, they seated themselves in the gallery to watch what would happen. Most senators, reading the petitions, grinned or laughed. When one sarcastically recommended that all the petitions be given to the Committee on Public Lands, the majority of the senators voted for this.

Since such a committee could do nothing for woman suffrage, Susan was angered. She went back to the convention and cried out to the women, "When you return home, get thousands of additional signatures on petitions. Keep sending them to Congress!"

And that is what the women did.

A year later, on January 10, 1878, the Honorable Aaron Sargent of California stood up in the Senate. Senator Sargent, who was Susan's close friend, introduced a proposal for a Sixteenth Amendment to the Constitution. The text was simple, using the language of the Fifteenth Amendment.

"The right of citizens of the United States to vote shall not be denied or abridged by the United States or by any State on account of sex."

This measure was received with respect and was referred to the proper committee. But after considering the proposed amendment the committee turned it down.

10. Going Forward

Every winter Susan spent some time in Washington. She lobbied at the Capitol, pleading for support for the woman suffrage amendment. She sorely missed Senator Sargent who was not reelected, but she made new friends in both the Senate and the House.

Susan went to these men at the beginning of each new term of Congress and appealed to them to reintroduce the amendment. When she could not find a senator or representative in his office, she searched him out at his home.

"I thought just as likely as not you would come fussing around . . . ," her good friend Senator Henry Blair of New Hampshire wrote to her one winter when she was pushing him for action. "I wish you would go home. . . . Go off and get married!"

The amendment was reintroduced in Congress again and again. In each chamber it was regularly referred to a committee. Susan persuaded the committees to hold hearings at the time of the annual convention of the National Woman Suffrage Association in Washington. Then she took the best speakers, including Mrs. Stanton, to address the committees.

One year, instead of the usual speakers, Susan took some of the fine young women she was now recruiting into the association. The Senate committee listened to them courteously, but after the hearing one senator spoke to Susan.

"Where are the old war horses? We want to hear those strong-minded women."

When Mrs. Stanton learned of this remark, she laughed heartily. And she said to Susan, "Well, you and I never sat like little birds on a limb singing, 'Suffrage, if you please.'"

The next day Mrs. Stanton and other long-time workers addressed the Senate committee.

Despite all these efforts, however, only once during the 1880s did the amendment advance from committee to a vote by the entire Senate. There it was hotly opposed and defeated. In the House during these same years, the amendment did not even once come up for a vote.

When Susan was 63 years old, she took the first real vacation of her life. One of the young workers persuaded Susan to accompany her to Europe as a companion, with expenses paid. Susan had a delightful time. And in England she talked with women who were also trying to win the right to vote in their country.

"How splendid it would be if women from many nations could gather together for an international conference," said Susan, a little breathless at the thought. Her new English friends liked the idea.

The large international conference was held in March 1888 at Washington, D.C., under the auspices of the National Woman Suffrage Association. Delegates came from Europe and Asia. Lucy Stone and other members of the American Woman Suffrage Association also attended. For the first time women from all parts of the world discussed their movement for equality.

Newspapers praised the conference highly. "What a change!" thought Susan. "I remember when the press had only ridicule for women's meetings."

Newspapers had high praise too for Susan, who presided at the meetings. Again Susan thought, "What a change!" She remembered when she was the laughingstock of the press.

Young members in both the National and American Associations enjoyed seeing the three pioneers together—Susan, Mrs. Stanton, and Lucy Stone. "Let us unite," pleaded the young people. "Both organizations have the same goal—votes for women."

Susan welcomed the union. Details were worked out, and in 1890 the two organizations merged under the name of the National American Woman Suffrage Association. Susan wanted Mrs. Stanton to be the first president.

"It is only right," she told the members. "Long ago at Seneca Falls she was the first woman in this nation to demand the vote for women." Mrs. Stanton was elected president of the unified, more powerful suffrage association.

Susan looked ahead with hope, telling herself, "Now women will give a strong pull and a pull all together for the vote."

11. President

In 1892 Susan was elected president of the united Woman Suffrage Association. Mrs. Stanton retired, and the following year Lucy Stone died.

When plans were made for a World's Fair at Chicago in 1893, Susan worked with influential leaders to make sure that women would have a prominent part. She herself attended and made numerous speeches. People now honored Susan as one of the nation's most distinguished citizens and crowded into auditoriums to hear her.

When some clergymen wanted the fair closed on Sundays, Susan spoke her mind. She pointed out that it was the only day many working people could attend.

"Would you like to have a son of yours go to Buffalo Bill's Wild West Show on Sunday?" an indignant clergyman asked Susan.

"Certainly," she replied.

The delighted Buffalo Bill sent her tickets for one

Election day in Wyoming. The woman suffrage movement won its first victory here.

of his performances. Susan went, accompanied by a group of young women. When Buffalo Bill rode into the arena, he made straight for her seat. Reining his prancing horse in front of Susan, he swept off his hat in a grand salute. Laughing, Susan rose and waved her handkerchief at Buffalo Bill. The crowd broke into wild applause.

From the fair Susan traveled to her home in Rochester. She and her sister Mary, a retired schoolteacher, now lived there together. Her other sisters and her mother were dead. Susan still kept in touch with her brothers in Kansas, and her nieces and nephews often visited the Rochester home.

Susan continued to work in states where woman suffrage came up for a vote. She had done this many times since that first campaign in Kansas, but there had been a series of defeats. Wyoming, in 1890, was the first state to give women the vote. During the 1890s victory came in three more states—Colorado, Idaho, and Utah.

Susan still kept pressure on Congress, for she held fast to her belief that votes for all women must come through a constitutional amendment. Susan resigned the presidency of the Woman Suffrage Association in 1900, when she was 80 years old. But she never stopped working for the amendment.

Addressing the association's national convention in February 1906, Susan said in a voice that was clear, though weak, "The fight must not cease! You must see that it does not stop!"

Instantly all the women were on their feet. For ten minutes they applauded and cheered their great pioneer leader. Many wept. They saw that Susan was very frail. As they looked upon her good face, now so pale, they felt that they were saying good-bye.

One month later Susan died. She was 86 years old.

Crusaders for the federal suffrage measure named it the Susan B. Anthony Amendment. It was passed in 1920, not as the Sixteenth Amendment for which Susan had labored, but as the Nineteenth Amendment. Exactly one hundred years after Susan's birth, women throughout the United States at last had the right to vote.

"I believe in equal rights," Susan had said at the beginning of her long courageous struggle. After winning suffrage, women still did not have total equality with men. When women later took up the fight for this goal, they were trying to finish the work that Susan and other pioneers had begun.

Eleanor Roosevelt
First Lady of the World

by Charles P. Graves

Copyright © 1966 by Charles P. Graves

1. Two Voyages

"Look, Eleanor." Mr. Roosevelt lifted his little girl above the ship's rail. "There's the Statue of Liberty. It was put up just last year."

Eleanor gazed at the giant statue of "Miss Liberty" holding a torch. The year was 1887. Anna Eleanor Roosevelt was two and a half years old. She and her mother and father were on the *Britannic*, a ship that was leaving New York City for Europe.

The next day the ship ran into some heavy fog. The fog whistle blew every few seconds to warn other ships nearby.

Mr. and Mrs. Roosevelt had tea with some friends that afternoon. Mrs. Roosevelt was a very lovely woman. She thought Eleanor was an ugly duckling. "She is such a funny child," Eleanor's mother said to one of her friends. "She's so shy and so old-fashioned. We call her 'Granny.'"

Eleanor hung her head in shame. She was glad when her parents took her for a walk on deck. The fog was so thick that Eleanor could hardly see the water. Suddenly the fog lifted. Another ship was headed straight toward them!

With a loud noise the ship plowed into the *Britannic*. It ripped a big hole in her side.

"Stay here," Mr. Roosevelt told his family. "I'll get our life preservers."

When he returned the deck was crowded with passengers. A sailor ran up. "Lower the lifeboats!" he shouted. "The ship is sinking!"

Mr. Roosevelt was afraid to climb into a lifeboat holding Eleanor for fear that he might drop her.

"Hold my little girl," he told one of the sailors. "Then hand her to me."

When he was in the lifeboat, he held out his arms. The sailor tossed Eleanor through the air, and her father caught her. Eleanor started to cry.

The ship that hit the *Britannic* was the *Celtic*. It didn't seem to be sinking, so the men in the lifeboat rowed toward it. Sailors on the *Celtic* lifted the Roosevelts aboard.

A short time later a message came from the *Britannic*. The captain said the ship would not sink after all. But it must return to New York for repairs. The *Celtic* was going to New York too, so the Roosevelts stayed on board.

When Eleanor was five, her mother and father took her on another voyage. Her new baby brother, Elliot Roosevelt, Jr., was along too. This time the ship reached Europe safely.

The Roosevelts went to Italy, where Eleanor's

father gave her a donkey. He hired a boy to lead the donkey while Eleanor rode on its back.

The boy led the donkey up a steep, rocky trail. They were gone a long time. When they returned the boy was riding on the donkey and Eleanor was leading it.

"Why aren't you riding the donkey?" Eleanor's father asked.

"Because the boy doesn't have any shoes," Eleanor said. "The rocks cut his feet, and they're bleeding. I've got shoes on, and I don't mind walking."

Mr. Roosevelt picked Eleanor up and hugged her. "I'm glad you're so kind and generous," he said.

Eleanor smiled. Her father always made her feel important and happy. Eleanor was never shy around him. She loved her father more than anyone else.

2. Orphans

While the Roosevelts were in Europe, another baby was born. They named him Hall.

When they returned to New York, Mr. and Mrs. Roosevelt went to many parties. One day Mr. Roosevelt asked Eleanor to go to a party. It was a Thanksgiving dinner for poor newsboys. Mr. Roosevelt wanted Eleanor to help serve the dinner at the newsboys' clubhouse.

As they rode there in a carriage, Mr. Roosevelt

said, "There are many poor people in the world. It is our duty to help them." He told Eleanor that many of the newsboys were orphans and had no homes.

"Where do they sleep?" Eleanor asked.

"Sometimes in wooden boxes," Mr. Roosevelt said. "Sometimes in the doorways of buildings."

When they reached the clubhouse, it was crowded with newsboys. Eleanor saw that many of them wore rags. She was pleased to help serve the dinner. The boys had all the turkey they could eat.

When the dinner was finished, the boys put on a show. One boy stood up and told a joke. "There are two good reasons why people don't mind their own business," he began. "One is that they have no business. The other is that they have no minds."

"Ha—ha!" Eleanor laughed loudly. All the newsboys looked at her. Eleanor blushed so red that her face looked like a ripe tomato. Eleanor was painfully shy, and she hated to call attention to herself.

The newsboys sang "Yankee Doodle," and Eleanor tried to sing with them. Then she fell sound asleep, and her father put her in the carriage.

The next morning Eleanor overslept and was late to school. This was unusual, for her school was on the top floor of her house. Her mother and some of her friends ran the school for their children.

Sometimes when the school day was over, Eleanor's mother read to her. One day she was too sick to

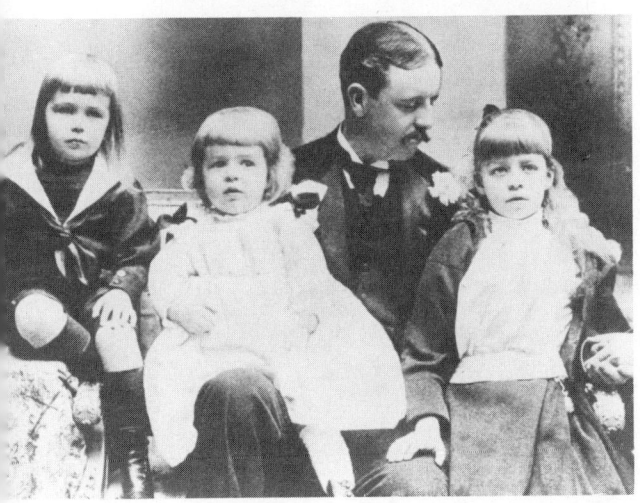

From Eleanor Roosevelt's photo album (counterclockwise): As a small girl; with Elliot firmly in tow; with papa, Elliot, and baby Hall; as a serious-minded young woman.

read. Doctors and nurses came to the house. The children had to be quiet all day.

Mrs. Roosevelt got worse. In a few days she died. Eleanor's father was overcome with sorrow. He could not take care of the children. Eleanor and her two brothers went to live with their grandmother.

The next spring there was more sorrow in the family. Elliot, Jr., became ill and died.

Mr. Roosevelt came to see Eleanor and Hall whenever he could. Sometimes he took her for a ride in the park. But he was not well. Before Eleanor was ten, her father died too.

Now Eleanor was an orphan.

3. Uncle Ted

Eleanor lived with her Grandmother Hall, who had one house in New York City and another one in the country. In the summer Eleanor often went to visit her father's brother, Theodore Roosevelt. She called him Uncle Ted. He lived in Oyster Bay, New York.

Uncle Ted had a big family of his own, and many nieces and nephews. The house was always full of children. Uncle Ted liked to play with the children and teach them sports.

Once the children were swimming in Oyster Bay. Uncle Ted saw Eleanor standing on the dock.

"Can't you swim, Eleanor?" Uncle Ted asked.
"No," Eleanor said.
"Well, jump off the dock and try."

Eleanor was afraid. But she finally got enough courage to jump. She went under the water and came up choking. Then Uncle Ted's children ducked her. Eleanor was terrified. But she loved Oyster Bay just the same.

When Eleanor was fifteen, the visits came to an end. Her grandmother sent her to England to school. Eleanor had never been to a real school. But she soon found that she liked it. She enjoyed being with the other girls and made many friends.

While in England, Eleanor heard some exciting news about Uncle Ted. He had been elected vice-president of the United States. William McKinley was the new president.

The next year more news came from America. President McKinley was killed by an assassin, and Uncle Ted became president.

When she was seventeen, Eleanor left school and returned to America. She was a tall, shy girl who was not at all pretty. She was not very popular at dances. But people who knew her well liked her because she was so honest and sincere.

One summer day she was riding on a train in New York State. A handsome young man came up to her. "Hello, Eleanor," he said. It was her distant cousin,

Eleanor Roosevelt in a picture taken on her wedding day, March 17, 1905.

Franklin D. Roosevelt. "My mother is in the next car," Franklin said. "Come say hello to her."

Franklin and his mother were going to their country home at Hyde Park.

"I remember the first time you came to Hyde Park," Franklin's mother told Eleanor. "You were just a baby."

In the months that followed, Eleanor began to see more of Franklin. They often went to parties and football games together. Franklin was a student at Harvard. He loved sports such as tennis and sailing.

When Eleanor was nineteen, Franklin asked her to marry him. "You won't even have to change your last name," Franklin said.

Eleanor said she'd be delighted to marry him. But Franklin's mother thought they were too young. She made them wait. Eleanor worked in a settlement house in New York helping the poor, while Franklin finished college.

In the fall of 1904, Mrs. Roosevelt let them announce their engagement. Another exciting thing happened that fall. Uncle Ted was elected to serve four more years as president. Eleanor asked him to give her away at her wedding.

Uncle Ted was a busy man. "I'm going to be in New York next St. Patrick's Day," he said. "Can you be married on March 17?"

"That's perfect," Eleanor said.

Early in March Uncle Ted was sworn in as president. Eleanor and Franklin went to Washington, D.C., to watch. They had seats just behind Uncle Ted. They listened to his speech. "We have duties to others and duties to ourselves, and we can shirk neither," they heard him say.

Two weeks later Eleanor and Franklin were married in the home of one of Eleanor's relatives. President Roosevelt, with Eleanor on his arm, came down the stairs.

Her wedding dress was made of white satin and lace. Her veil was decorated with orange blossoms and fastened with a diamond pin. Franklin met her at the altar.

"Dearly beloved . . . ," the minister began. When he came to the words, "Who giveth this woman to be married to this man?" all the wedding guests leaned forward.

Uncle Ted was supposed to push Eleanor gently ahead and place her hand in the minister's hand. Instead, he said, "I do," in a loud voice.

Finally the minister pronounced Franklin and Eleanor man and wife, and the reception began. Most of the guests paid little attention to the bride and groom. They crowded around the president.

"You'd think he was the bride," Franklin said with a grin. Eleanor didn't mind. Soon she and Franklin were crowding around Uncle Ted too.

4. A Busy Life

Franklin's mother was a rich and strong-willed woman. She still tried to make all the decisions for Franklin and Eleanor, just as if they were children.

Both Franklin and Eleanor called her "mama." Mama expected them to spend a great deal of time with her. She gave them a house in New York City where she also had a home. Eleanor saw her every day.

Eleanor told her that she was expecting a baby. "We'll name him James," mama said, "after my husband."

But the baby was a girl. Eleanor named her Anna Eleanor.

The next year the Roosevelts had a son, and mama had her way. They named him James. Two years later another boy was born and named Franklin, Jr. He was a big, beautiful baby, but when he was a few months old, he became sick and died. Franklin helped Eleanor get over her grief.

Franklin worked in a law office. One night he told Eleanor that he didn't like his job.

"Uncle Ted says that the best work a man can do is to help his fellow men. I'd like to go into politics."

"Fine," Eleanor said. "If that's what you want to do, go ahead."

Franklin ran for state senator of New York on the Democratic ticket. No one thought he had much chance to win. The voters in his district were almost all Republicans.

Eleanor couldn't help him as she had a new baby and had to stay home. The baby was a boy and was called Elliot after Eleanor's father.

Franklin worked hard to win votes. He went out and met the people in his district. They liked him. The election was close, but Franklin was the winner.

In 1912 Franklin helped Woodrow Wilson run for president of the United States. Wilson won and made Franklin the assistant secretary of the navy. This was an important job. Uncle Ted had been assistant secretary of the navy before he became president.

Eleanor and Franklin moved their children to Washington, D.C. Franklin often had to go on trips to inspect navy bases and ships. Sometimes Eleanor went with him.

Once she rode on a battleship that was towing a target for other ships to shoot at. The ship rose and fell on the waves. Eleanor felt seasick. She was afraid she was going to disgrace her husband.

A naval officer came up to her and pointed to the mast. "You could see the gunfire much better up there," he said. "Wouldn't you like to climb up?"

"I couldn't feel any worse up there than I do down here," Eleanor thought. The mast was as tall as a five-story building. It took her a long time to reach the top. Once she was there, her seasickness left her. She had a fine view of the target practice.

While Franklin was assistant secretary of the navy, the Roosevelts had two more children: Franklin D. Roosevelt, Jr., and John.

Franklin's mother had given them a summer home on Campobello Island in Canada. In 1916 Eleanor took the children there for the summer. There was a terrible polio epidemic in the United States.

Franklin had to be in Washington. He wrote that the polio epidemic was "appalling." He was so worried about his children's health that he wouldn't let Eleanor bring them back until the epidemic was over.

He was also worried about the war that was going on in Europe. In 1917 America entered World War I on the side of the Allies, fighting Germany.

Eleanor did a great deal of war work. She spent two or three days a week at a Red Cross canteen near the railroad station. She would help make sandwiches and coffee to give to the soldiers who came through Washington. Afterward she often mopped the floor of the canteen.

Many soldiers and sailors who were wounded in the war were brought to hospitals in Washington. Eleanor visited them often and brought presents.

The Roosevelts at Campobello: Franklin, Eleanor, Anna, and mama. Below, several years later, Eleanor, Franklin D., Jr., Elliot, and Anna.

Later she almost turned her own home into a hospital. Her husband and all five children came down with the flu at the same time. She nursed them all. She cooked their meals, made their beds, gave them their baths, and took their temperatures.

Someone asked her how she managed, and she said, "I learned that what one has to do can be done."

5. Polio and Politics

In 1920 Franklin was nominated to run for vice-president of the United States. This meant that he was one of the most important men in America. Politicians came to see him at all hours of the day and night.

One night several famous people came to dinner. Eleanor couldn't think of anything to say. She went upstairs to put the children to bed. While hearing their prayers, she burst into tears. She stayed upstairs for a long time.

Franklin came up to see what was wrong.

"I just can't stand to greet all those people," Eleanor sobbed. "I know they think I'm dull and unattractive. I just want to hide up here."

"I think you're beautiful," Franklin said, "especially when you're wearing an evening dress. Come on back downstairs."

Eleanor went and did her best.

One man who came to the house a lot was Franklin's friend and assistant, Louis Howe. At first Eleanor didn't like Louis. He was an untidy little man who smoked all the time. Louis worked hard on Franklin's speeches, and Franklin thought he was a genius. Eleanor began to respect him.

But nothing Howe or Roosevelt did could win enough votes that year. The people liked the Republican candidate for president, Warren G. Harding. The Democrats were beaten. But Louis Howe wasn't discouraged. He passed the White House and said, "That's where Franklin is going someday."

The next summer the Roosevelts went to Campobello Island as usual. They had a sailboat named the *Vireo*.

One afternoon Franklin and the three oldest children were out in the boat. Anna was fifteen now. As the *Vireo* skimmed through the water, the Roosevelts saw a forest fire on another island. They landed and fought the fire. Then they returned to Campobello.

"Let's go for a swim," Franklin said. They took a quick dip, and the water felt like ice.

When they came home, Franklin had a chill. The next day he was sick. His legs became paralyzed. Eleanor was terribly worried about him, but she tried not to show it.

Several doctors came to see Franklin. They didn't

know what was wrong. There were no nurses on the island. Eleanor took care of him all day long. She slept on a couch in Franklin's room.

Then another doctor came to see Franklin. He said he was sure Franklin had polio. Franklin and Eleanor were afraid the children might catch the disease. But none did.

After he got better, Franklin was taken to New York. But he was badly crippled. He could not move his legs. His mother wanted him to come to Hyde Park and live there as an invalid the rest of his life. She said she would take care of him.

Now for the first time Eleanor had the courage to disagree with Franklin's mother. "He must learn to take care of himself," she said. "He can still lead a useful life."

Louis Howe agreed with Eleanor. He still thought Franklin would be president someday. But Franklin was discouraged. He had loved sports. Now he couldn't even walk.

"We must get him interested in politics again," Louis said.

"How?" Eleanor asked.

"You must go into politics," Louis said. "That will get him interested again."

Eleanor started to work in the women's division of the Democratic State Committee. She brought politicians home with her to talk to Franklin. Sometimes when he talked politics, he would forget that he was crippled. And Eleanor would forget that she was shy. She was getting more and more interested in politics.

Eleanor had to make some speeches. This was very hard for her. But she made herself do it. Louis Howe helped. He listened to her practice her speeches and showed her how she could be a better speaker.

She went to the New York State Democratic Convention in 1928. The governor of New York was Alfred E. Smith. He was going to run for president.

Smith wanted Eleanor to persuade Franklin to run for governor of New York.

"He must make his own decisions," Eleanor said. Franklin was in Warm Springs, Georgia. Swimming in the warm water there made him feel better. He still thought he might learn to walk again if he took good care of himself.

"We've tried to call him in Georgia," Smith said. "But he won't come to the phone. Will you try?"

"I'll try," Eleanor said, "but I won't try to make him change his mind."

Eleanor finally reached Franklin. "Governor Smith wants to talk to you," she said. She handed the phone to Smith and rushed out of the room to catch a train.

The next morning she read in the papers that Franklin had agreed to run for governor. It was another close election, but Franklin won. The Roosevelts moved to the big Executive Mansion in Albany.

Anna was married now and had a baby. The boys were away at school and college. But when they came to Albany on weekends, they made the Executive Mansion a lively place.

6. The White House

While Roosevelt was governor of New York, a terrible economic depression hit the United States. Businesses went broke. Millions of men lost their jobs. Many people didn't have enough to eat.

Mrs. Roosevelt got many letters from poor people. One old woman wrote that she was all alone except for her little dog. Now the dog was about to be taken away from her because she was too poor to pay the tax on it. Mrs. Roosevelt paid the tax, and the old woman kept her dog.

The depression became worse and worse. Banks failed, and people lost all their money. More and more workers lost their jobs. Mrs. Roosevelt's heart went out to these people. She told beggars she met on the street that they could get free meals at her house. She found jobs for many worthy people.

Eleanor was busier than ever. She taught history and government in a girls' school in New York City.

She also helped her husband in his work as governor. She traveled about the state and visited reform schools, hospitals, and prisons. Then she would tell her husband what was wrong with them. He tried to make them better places.

He also tried to end the depression in New York State. But the depression was all over the country. It could not be ended in New York unless it was ended in the other states.

Franklin began to think that if he were president, he could put an end to the depression throughout the nation.

Louis Howe wanted him to run for president. So did many other leaders in the Democratic party. So Roosevelt was nominated for president at the Democratic convention in Chicago. He and Eleanor flew to Chicago. As they entered the convention hall, the delegates cheered wildly.

Franklin went all over America on a campaign train. He wanted to talk to as many people as he could. Eleanor traveled with him part of the time. Everywhere the Roosevelts went, the bands played Franklin's campaign song, "Happy Days Are Here Again." The voters believed Franklin could bring happy days back to America. They elected him by millions of votes.

As soon as Franklin was elected, a reporter asked Eleanor what she was thinking.

"I am happy for my husband," she said, "because in many ways it makes up for the blow he suffered when he was stricken with infantile paralysis. And I have confidence in his ability to help the country. . . ."

Now it was Franklin's turn to be inaugurated just as Uncle Ted had been so many years before. On inauguration day, Eleanor rode from the White House to the Capitol with Mrs. Hoover, the wife of the outgoing president.

Mrs. Roosevelt wore a blue dress which the newspaper reporters called "Eleanor blue." The crowds cheered and waved as she went by. Eleanor waved back at the people.

After the inauguration there was a big parade. Eleanor watched it from a reviewing stand. Thousands of soldiers marched by.

The Roosevelts moved into the White House. Eleanor was determined to make it as comfortable and informal as possible. She insisted on running the White House elevator herself. "That just isn't done, Mrs. Roosevelt," a servant said.

"It is now," Eleanor replied with a smile.

Sometimes Eleanor took visitors on a tour of the White House. "My feeling about the White House is that it belongs to the people," she said. "Their taxes support it. . . . they should be made to feel welcome here."

7. First Lady in America

President Roosevelt had promised the people that he would try to end the depression. He asked Congress to pass laws that helped banks, businesses, farmers, and workers. The government hired people who were without jobs. These people built roads, dams, parks, and public buildings.

Because the president was crippled, it was hard for him to travel. But he needed firsthand information about the country. So he asked Eleanor to be his eyes and ears—and especially his legs.

Eleanor had overcome her shyness. She gladly tackled the job. No other first lady had ever worked so closely with her husband.

"I've heard that there is terrible poverty in the mining towns of West Virginia," Franklin said to Eleanor. "I want you to go there and then come back and tell me the truth."

Eleanor was shocked at what she saw in West Virginia. Some of the men had been out of work for years. Even those with jobs were paid only a few dollars a week.

Eleanor visited many of the poor people. There were six children in one of the families. The father said he had only a dollar a week to feed them. Eleanor noticed that the children ate scraps out of a bowl, just like dogs.

As she was leaving, Eleanor saw a little boy holding a pet rabbit in his arms.

"What a cute rabbit!" she said. But the boy seemed afraid.

His older sister said, "He thinks we are not going to eat it. But we'll have to." The boy ran out of the house, holding his rabbit tight against his chest.

When Eleanor returned to Washington, she told this story at a White House dinner. The next day she received a check from one of the guests. A note said the check was to help save the rabbit.

Eleanor did everything she could to help other people. She made a lot of money by writing a newspaper column called "My Day." She gave most of the money to the poor. And she told her husband how she thought he could help. Some of his ideas for ending the depression came from her.

Not everybody liked Mrs. Roosevelt, though. Some people thought she should stay home in the White House and mind her own business. But she felt that helping the people *was* her business.

Millions of Americans loved Mrs. Roosevelt. She seemed to be everywhere all the time. Her heart was big enough for all the people in the world.

A story is told about a little girl who had heard a great deal about Mrs. Roosevelt but had never seen her. The girl's mother took her to the Statue of Liberty one day.

"Do you know who that is?" her mother asked, pointing to the giant statue.

"Of course," the little girl replied, "that's Mrs. Roosevelt."

8. Third Term

Mrs. Roosevelt was now a very fine politician. She was a good public speaker, and she made friends easily. She helped her husband run for reelection in 1936. One important man called her "the most practical woman I've ever met in politics."

Roosevelt was reelected by one of the greatest majorities in American history.

One Republican said, "It isn't fair for the president to cash in on his own popularity and his wife's too."

Most Americans were proud of the Roosevelts when the king and queen of England came to visit them. Mrs. Roosevelt planned to have a picnic for them at Hyde Park.

"What are you going to serve?" a reporter asked.

"Probably hot dogs," Eleanor said.

Many people thought hot dogs were not fancy enough for a king and queen. But Mrs. Roosevelt went on with her plans. Someone told her that the king had never eaten a hot dog, but that he would like to try one.

A president's eyes and ears: visiting underground in a coal mine; hitting the campaign trail with FDR.

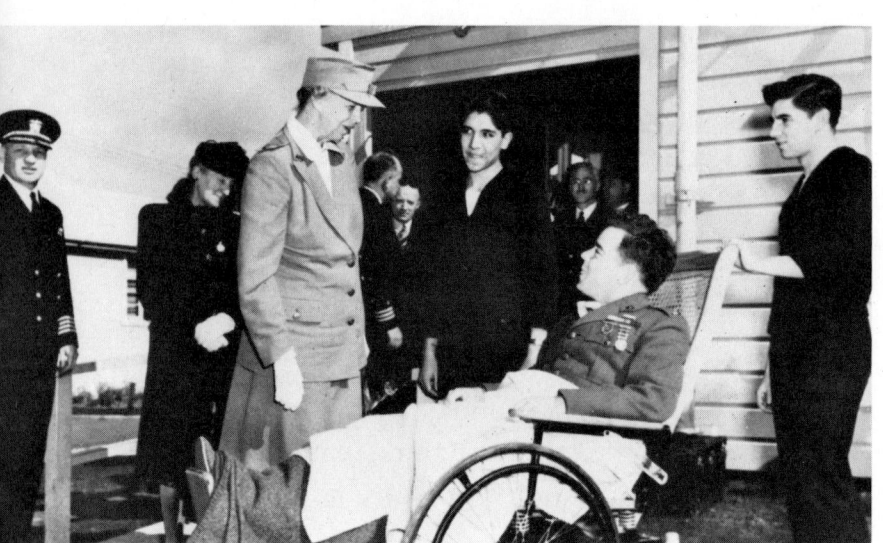

Cheering a wounded marine in the South Pacific

Entertaining the king and queen of England

At the picnic the king and queen ate hot dogs and seemed to like them. Afterward the president and the king went swimming, while the queen and Eleanor talked about their children.

The visit of the king and queen helped America and England become firm friends. A few months later World War II started. England was fighting Germany.

No one was sure whether or not America could keep out of the war. Because of the war, Roosevelt decided to run for a third term as president.

In all American history, no president had ever served more than two terms. There was no law against it, but many people thought it would be wrong.

During the campaign Eleanor was criticized by many Republicans. Some of them wore big buttons which said, "We don't want Eleanor either."

Someone asked Eleanor how she felt about the buttons. She laughed. "If I could be worried about mudslinging, I would have been dead long ago."

Roosevelt was easily elected for a third term. But he made many enemies. Some people tried to strike at him through Mrs. Roosevelt.

Once, after making a speech, she said she would be glad to answer questions.

"Mrs. Roosevelt," a man said, "do you think your husband's being a cripple has affected his mind?"

The man was trying to insult Mrs. Roosevelt, but she refused to be insulted.

"Yes," she said, "my husband's illness has affected him.... Suffering has made him more sensitive, more responsive to his fellow men."

Mrs. Roosevelt's quiet dignity won her more friends than ever.

9. World War II

On December 7, 1941, Japanese planes bombed American ships in Hawaii. Japan, Italy, and Germany declared war on the United States. Now America was in World War II.

All four of Mrs. Roosevelt's sons were in the armed forces. She was worried about them. But she knew the war had to be fought and won.

Queen Elizabeth asked Mrs. Roosevelt to come to England to see what English women were doing to win the war. The president thought this was a good idea. Eleanor could visit American troops there.

Mrs. Roosevelt flew to Ireland, then took a boat to England and a train to London. The king and queen met her at the railroad station and took her to Buckingham Palace.

The dinner at the palace that night was served on gold and silver plates. But food was scarce in England, and the meal was simple.

The king and queen took Eleanor on a trip around London. She saw many buildings that had been wrecked by German bombs.

Some people thought the Germans might try to kill Mrs. Roosevelt if they knew she was in England. So she was given a secret name. It was "Rover."

Mrs. Roosevelt's son Elliot was stationed at an airfield near London. A man drove Mrs. Roosevelt to see him. On the way they got lost. Someone with them called the American Embassy in London. He said, "Rover has lost her pup." The embassy gave him directions, and Rover had a joyful visit with her "pup."

Mrs. Roosevelt visited English factories where women were making bombs and airplanes. She went to see American soldiers who were in training camps. They cheered when they saw her.

The next year Mrs. Roosevelt went to the South Pacific. She visited homesick soldiers in hospitals. She signed her name on many bandages and casts. She wrote down the names of mothers, sweethearts, and wives and promised to telephone them when she returned to America. After she talked to one soldier, he turned to a friend. "Jeepers! She's just like your own mother."

Mrs. Roosevelt visited a cemetery on Guadalcanal where American soldiers were buried. She made up her mind that when the war was over, she would work for lasting peace. "I kept praying that I might be able to prevent . . . this stupidity called war," she said later.

When she returned to Washington, she spent many hours calling friends and relatives of soldiers she had met. One soldier had given her a message for the girl he planned to marry. Mrs. Roosevelt called and said, "This is Mrs. Roosevelt."

"Don't be funny," the girl said. "Who do you think you're fooling?" The girl would not believe it wasn't a joke. Mrs. Roosevelt finally had to write her a note.

President Roosevelt had worked long and hard for his country. He was tired. But he wanted to serve until the war was won. Then he wanted to help organize the United Nations. He hoped it would prevent future wars. So he ran for a fourth term as president and was elected.

The next spring he went to Warm Springs, Georgia, for a rest. Mrs. Roosevelt stayed in Washington. One day when she was away from the White House, she got a message asking her to return at once. When she reached the White House, she was told that her husband had died suddenly.

Mrs. Roosevelt did not think of herself. The country came first. She sent for Vice-President Harry Truman, who would now be the president.

"Harry, the president is dead," she told him.

"Is there anything I can do for you?" Truman asked.

"Is there anything we can do for you?" Mrs. Roosevelt answered. "For you are the one in trouble now."

Mrs. Roosevelt's job in the White House was finished. She had been first lady for more than twelve years. No other woman had ever been America's first lady for so long.

10. First Lady of the World

Late in 1945 President Truman asked Mrs. Roosevelt to be a United States delegate to the new United Nations. She accepted. She thought the United Nations was man's only hope for peace.

Mrs. Roosevelt was made chairman of the United Nations Commission for Human Rights. Her job was to help write a bill of rights for the people of the world.

A Russian member of the commission liked to make long speeches and slow the work down. Once he accused the United States of doing bad things.

Mrs. Roosevelt banged on the table for order. "We are here," she said sternly, "to devise ways of safeguarding human rights. We are not here to attack each other's governments. . . ."

Finally the bill was finished. It was called the

Declaration of Human Rights. When it was passed by the United Nations, all the delegates stood up and cheered Mrs. Roosevelt. People began to call her the First Lady of the World.

Mrs. Roosevelt also worked for the American Association for the United Nations. It tried to make Americans support the United Nations.

"It is not perfect," she said, "but it is all we have." As long as men argued with words, she thought, they would not fight with bullets.

Once she went to Russia and talked with Nikita Khrushchev, the head of the Russian government. They argued about many things.

As she left, he asked, "Can I tell our papers that we had a friendly conversation?"

"You can say that we had a friendly conversation, but that we differ," she told him.

"At least we didn't shoot each other," the Russian said with a grin.

Mrs. Roosevelt traveled all over the world in the cause of peace. People everywhere loved her. Strangers would come up and shake her hand. "Hi, Eleanor," they would say.

Mrs. Roosevelt was busy each day from breakfast to bedtime. She answered every letter she received— and there were thousands. She made speeches and wrote books. She helped the needy. And she helped the Democratic party.

Eleanor Roosevelt: United Nations delegate, chairman of the Human Rights Commission, first lady of the world.

Her friends tried to make her stop working so hard. But she wouldn't stop. "There's so much to do," she said.

In the fall of 1962, Mrs. Roosevelt became sick and went to a hospital. Everybody was worried about her. People felt better when she was able to leave the hospital and go home. But suddenly she became ill again. She died on November 7.

The whole world mourned. Many people who had never met her felt that they had lost a good friend.

The United Nations stopped its work in her honor. One of her great admirers made a speech. "Her glow has warmed the world," he said.

Index

A

American Anti-Slavery Society, 69, 104
American Woman Suffrage Association, 117, 124, 129
Anthony, Daniel, 88, 93, 109
Anthony, Guelma, 88, 91, 93, 119
Anthony, Hannah, 88, 93, 119
Anthony, Mary, 88, 119, 132
Anthony, Merritt, 88, 109
Anthony, Susan B., 86 (pic), 103 (pic), 125 (pic)
   and antislavery movement, 104-105, 106
   arrest and trial of, 120-122
   birth of, 87
   childhood of, 87, 88, 89
   death of, 133
   education of, 90, 91
   and National American Woman Suffrage Association, 130, 132
   and the *Revolution*, 113, 114, 115, 116, 117, 118, 119
   as teacher, 90, 92, 94
   and woman's rights, 97, 98, 100, 101, 102, 104, 110-112, 113, 114, 115, 116, 118, 122, 127, 129
   and Women's National Loyal League, 108
Antislavery movement, 63, 64, 66, 69, 70 (pic), 73, 82, 94, 104, 105, 106

B

Bloomer, Amelia, 81, 98 (pic)

C

Coffin, Lucretia. *See* Mott, Lucretia
Cotton, John, 15, 16, 20, 21, 23, 24, 25, 33

D

Declaration of Rights for Women, 123
Douglass, Frederick, 85, 94

F

Forten, James, 65

G

Garrison, William Lloyd, 63, 64, 69

H

Howe, Louis, 149, 150, 151, 153
Hutchinson, Anne, 6 (pic)
   birth of, 8, 9
   childhood of, 7, 8, 9, 10, 11
   death of, 46
   imprisonment of, 34-36
   goes to New England, 16, 17, 18
   preaches, 19, 24
   becomes a Puritan, 15
   settles in Rhode Island, 39 (pic), 40
   trial of, 29-31, 32 (pic), 33
Hutchinson, Edward (son of Anne Hutchinson), 21, 22, 37, 39
Hutchinson, Richard (son of Anne Hutchinson), 21
Hutchinson, Susanna (daughter of Anne Hutchinson), 45, 46
Hutchinson, Will (husband of Anne Hutchinson), 7, 8, 12, 16, 22, 23, 36, 37, 39, 40, 41

L

Lundy, Benjamin, 60-61

M

Marbury, Anne. *See* Hutchinson, Anne
Mott, Anna (daughter of Lucretia Mott), 59
Mott, Elizabeth (daughter of Lucretia Mott), 61
Mott, James (husband of Lucretia Mott), 56, 57, 58, 59, 61, 67 (pic), 68, 71, 73, 82, 84
Mott, Lucretia, 48 (pic), 67 (pic)
   and Susan B. Anthony, 81, 84
   goes to antislavery meeting in England, 69-70, 71, 72
   and antislavery work, 61, 62 (pic), 63, 64, 69, 70-72, 73, 74 (pic), 75, 76, 82, 83
   birth of, 50
   childhood of, 49-53

death of, 85
education of, 54, 55-56
marriage of, 58
and Philadelphia Female
    Anti-Slavery Society, 65-66
as Quaker preacher, 60, 62
starts school for blacks, 65, 66
as teacher, 57, 58, 59
and Underground Railroad, 73
and woman's rights, 76, 77, 78, 79-80, 85, 95
Mott, Maria (daughter of Lucretia Mott), 61
Mott, Martha (daughter of Lucretia Mott), 61
Mott, Thomas (son of Lucretia Mott), 59, 60

N

National American Woman Suffrage Association, 129
National Woman Suffrage Association, 117 (pic), 123, 124-125, 127, 129

P

Philadelphia Female Anti-Slavery Society, 65, 83
Puritans, 15, 16, 17 (pic), 26, 29, 42, 47

Q

Quakers, 51, 52, 60, 61, 64, 73, 91

R

Revolution, The, 113, 114, 115, 116, 117, 118, 119
Roosevelt, Anna Eleanor, 134 (pic), 139 (pic)
  as husband's aide, 150, 153, 155
  childhood of, 135-138, 139 (pic), 140
  as newspaper columnist, 156
  death of, 165
  and Declaration of Human Rights, 164
  education of, 138, 141
  visits wartime England, 160-161

and father, 135, 136, 137-138, 140
marriage of, 142 (pic), 143-144
becomes active in politics, 150-151
and concern for poor, 152, 155-156
tours South Pacific, 161-162
as teacher, 152
travels in the cause of peace, 164
as delegate to United Nations, 163-164, 165 (pic)
and war work, 147
Roosevelt, Anna Eleanor (daughter of Eleanor Roosevelt), 145, 149, 152
Roosevelt, Elliot (son of Eleanor Roosevelt), 145, 161
Roosevelt, Elliot, Jr., 136, 139 (pic), 140
Roosevelt, Franklin D. (husband of Eleanor Roosevelt), 142, 143, 144, 145, 146, 147 (pic), 148, 149-150, 151-152, 153
Roosevelt, Franklin D., Jr. (son of Eleanor Roosevelt), 146
Roosevelt, Franklin, Jr. (son of Eleanor Roosevelt), 145
Roosevelt, Hall, 137, 140
Roosevelt, James (son of Eleanor Roosevelt), 145
Roosevelt, John (son of Eleanor Roosevelt), 146
Roosevelt, Theodore, 140, 141, 143, 145-146

S

Slavery, 60, 61, 62, 63
Stanton, Elizabeth Cady, 72, 76, 77, 78, 79, 80, 81, 84, 95, 96, 103 (pic), 108, 110, 112, 113, 114, 116, 123, 127, 128, 129-130
Stone, Lucy, 96, 97, 98, 99, 103 (pic), 111, 113, 116, 117, 124, 129, 130
Symmes, Zachariah, 19, 20, 23, 34, 35

U

Underground Railroad, 73
United Nations, 162, 163, 164, 165
United Nations Commission for Human Rights, 163

167

W

Williams, Roger, 31, 36, 39
Wilson, John, 23, 24, 26, 27, 28, 31, 35, 36, 37, 38, 42, 47
Winthrop, John, 27, 28 (pic), 30, 32, 33, 38, 40
Woman's Journal, 117
Woman's rights movement
  aims of, 72, 77, 78, 79, 93, 96, 100, 104
  beginnings in antislavery movement, 60–66, 71–72, 75, 81–82, 94, 95, 104–106
  conventions of, 77–79, 85, 95, 104
  leaders of, 72, 76–77, 81, 100, 117, 123, 129
  opposition to, 71, 79–80, 95, 97–100, 101
Woman's suffrage
  demand for, 83–84, 96, 97, 100, 102, 110, 114, 117 (pic)
  granted, 131 (pic), 133
  opposition to, 101, 110
  support of, 111–112, 113, 114, 126
Women's National Loyal League, 108, 109
Working Women's Association, 116
World War I, 147
World War II, 159, 160, 161